THE
FAIRY GOD DOCTOR'S
Guide to a Good Life
A Prescription for the Working Woman

DR. DENISE BROWN

LEGACY
launch pad
PUBLISHING

The Fairy God Doctor's Guide to a Good Life: A Prescription for the Working Woman

Copyright © 2025 by Denise S. Brown, MD

ISBN:

978-1-964377-61-2 (paperback)

978-1-964377-62-9 (hardcover)

978-1-964377-63-6 (ebook)

Published by Legacy Launch Pad Publishing

First Edition

Download the Fairy God Doctor's daily prescription for a good life by scanning the QR code below:

ADVANCE PRAISE FOR DENISE BROWN AND
THE FAIRY GOD DOCTOR'S GUIDE TO A GOOD LIFE

"This book is a giant breath of fresh air, offering women an uplifting and practical approach to create the lives they love versus getting trapped in the lives they 'should' be living. I only wish Dr. Denise had been by my side earlier in my career. You can bet I'm getting a copy of this book for my daughter and every one of her friends!"

—Nataly Kogan, bestselling author of
Happier Now and *The Awesome Human Project*

"Dr. Denise tackles a fundamental issue for women in a way that only she can; she dazzles with her iconic humor and wit, grabs you with stories that tug at your heartstrings and shares examples from her own life to show you that inward is the way. As someone who teaches on soul-care, loving yourself radically and finding what sets your soul on fire, this book thrills me to my marrow. Until you heal and sit with little you, tell her she is enough and make good with your own soul, none of the worldly accolades will hit the *real* targets: your heart, mind and soul. I can't wait to hear from the army of women who get *unburdened* from expectations because of this book."

— Rachel Joy Baribeau, bestselling author of *Relentless Joy*,
founder of ImChangingtheNarrative.org,
former national sportscaster and Heisman voter

"A fairy godmother helps you see what truly matters and frees you to live life on your terms. This book does the same by flipping the script on success, trading guilt for self-trust and pressure for purpose, and sharing that the 'magic' you need already exists inside you. Dr. Denise gives you the precise prescription to be free of others' expectations and comparisons, to be happy and to make the bold choice to own your path today."

—Leigh Burgess, *USA Today* bestselling author of *Be BOLD Today: Unleash Your Potential, Master Your Mindset, and Achieve Success.*

"Many, many years ago, a young girl became a student in my ninth grade honors English class. Denise was a bright, shining star and continues to be such. *The Fairy God Doctor's Guide to a Good Life* is her first attempt to write for the public, and she wrote the story she lived. Bless her heart and do not miss this book!"

—Barbara Fernelius, high school English teacher for 45+ years (and Denise's favorite)

"My 20-something daughter and I have a mantra: 'What would Denise do?' Through 15 years of friendship with Denise, we have seen how she navigates challenging people and situations with grace, humour and clear-eyed intelligence. I am thrilled that her wisdom, energy and life experience can now be shared more widely. This is the friend every young woman needs, and this is the book I wish I'd had in my twenties."

—Jessica Davies London-based author,
journalist and family therapist

"*The Fairy God Doctor's Guide to a Good Life* gives us the warm feeling of sitting down with your funny older sister over a glass of wine. Dr. Denise Brown knows how to deliver both advice and laughs in the way we all want and need in life."

—Robin Dybevik, Creative Marketing Executive at Netflix

DEDICATION

"There are only two lasting bequests we can give our children—
one is roots, the other, wings."

–Henry Ward Beecher

For Big Mama, who gave me both

TABLE OF CONTENTS

PREFACE

Losing my mom at 25 felt like the rug had been pulled out from under me. Suddenly, I had no one to confide in or ask for advice. That forced me to think carefully about my life, to be ruthless with my priorities and to make everything count. Mom's death at just 53 years old gave me two gifts: the ability to see the big picture and the realization that I didn't have time to waste. I had to become my own woman instantly; that was the most painful and lasting kindness she gave me.

I wrote this book because I see so many women feeling lost and overwhelmed, especially those in their late 20s who are just starting their careers and adult lives. These women try to make everyone happy and do all the "right" things, but they're often left feeling adrift, wondering if they're on the best path. I know that sensation all too well, and I wish I'd had someone to turn to back then. This book is my way of offering that big-sister guidance and sharing the insights I've gained over the years.

This book is my legacy, an idea that came up unexpectedly in a conversation one day. A friend asked me about my lasting impact, and I instinctively thought of my two kids and my journey with work and family. But as I reflected, I realized that my legacy wasn't just about my children. It was about the joy I found in raising them, building a career and cherishing my friendships.

That conversation sparked the idea for this project. As I look back, I realize I have always loved talking to women who are just starting out on their journeys—because I remember feeling unmoored, trying to please everyone while wondering if I've made the right choices.

I don't know if anyone is qualified to write a book, but I did run a medical practice, a strategic practice and a company. By any objective measure of career success, all my boxes are ticked. I've built a thriving career, raised two incredible boys who are delightedly feminist even if they don't want to admit it and maintained a long and happy marriage. I've also enjoyed the privilege of being surrounded by a supportive network of friends and family who've helped me along the way.

Privilege plays a significant role in my story, and I'm acutely aware of it. I had the advantage of being born into a loving, well-educated family that broke gender norms early on. This gave me confidence and offered me opportunities that many others didn't have. But privilege isn't just about where you're born or who your parents are; it's about who loves you and who you're surrounded by. I feel incredibly blessed in all these areas, which is why I feel a responsibility to share what I've learned.

This book is not for women in the medical profession or for those who want to be mothers. It's for every woman trying to figure out what matters most to her and how to navigate the pressures of life without giving a f*** about what the rest of the world thinks. It's about Katilyn, who grew up with a dream of having twins but can't realize it with the $212,000 she owes in school debt. Or maybe Jeanne, who wants wholeheartedly to dedicate her time to her advertising career but listens to her mom begging for grandkids every weekend. This book is about Peyton, who has a four-year-old in daycare and is so riddled with guilt that she's sick to her stomach all day at work. It's about making conscious choices that align with your true self and living a life that's authentically yours.

It is my passionate (and sometimes nearly manic) hope that this book will help you find satisfaction your way!

I want you to make choices that align with your values and enjoy a life well-lived. Someday, I want us all to be delighted little old ladies, sitting in our rocking chairs, sipping margaritas and knowing that we did it right—that we lived fully and authentically as satisfied working women.

ORIGINS OF THE FAIRY GOD DOCTOR

The secrets of Los Alamos shaped my childhood.

L os Alamos lies in a quiet, windswept corner of northern New Mexico. During World War II, it was transformed into a secret laboratory, hidden from the world, where some of the brightest scientific minds worked tirelessly to develop the atomic bomb. Tucked between mountains, the makeshift town buzzed with activity as scientists, engineers and military personnel collaborated in a high-stakes race against Nazi Germany. Of course, you've heard of its most famous effort, the Manhattan Project, which culminated in the first successful atomic explosion in July 1945. Today, it reminds us of the shadow side of scientific brilliance and all its moral dilemmas. Both of my parents worked there, so I grew up in Los Alamos. It was weird.

In this mini-memoir, I'll tell you the story of a young woman grappling with agonizing decisions through the rigors of medical training, tragedy and motherhood—all while holding together a career and home. It's a story of resilience, adaptability and the power of seeking and offering support. This book is not about success, because we all want something more than that—something better. My experiences sent me in search of satisfaction, and satisfaction is the bedrock of the advice in this book.

Youth

My childhood home, despite the strange bubble in Los Alamos, was a place of comfort. I had a younger brother and loving parents, and as the eldest daughter of top-secret scientists, my life was enveloped by a sense of mystery and a love for the intellectual. Both of my parents held prestigious positions at the Los Alamos National Lab. Due to their classified clearances, conversations about work were off-limits, and the air was always thick with secrets. Like many other parents in our town, my mom and dad couldn't discuss their jobs, even amongst themselves. We were in the middle of nowhere, surrounded by other scientists' families who were shrouded by the same veil of secrecy. The standard answer to, "What do your parents do?" was simply, "They work at the lab."

School was my arena. I skipped kindergarten and quickly established myself as one of the smart kids. By sixth grade, our self-paced math program became a student battleground, and the ultimate prize was to reach algebra first. I was confident I was in the lead—until I was blindsided by a boy named Alex who beat me by nearly three months! This unassuming boy, who had quietly shared a classroom with me since third grade, suddenly emerged as my fiercest competitor. He was so short! He had a head of wavy brown hair and dark green eyes that hid behind his 1980s glasses. At 11 years old, Alex Brown had bested me in math and emerged as a significant figure in my life. By the end of sixth grade, Alex and the rest of our dorky group spent countless hours engrossed in board games. Risk and Diplomacy, our favorites, became a new way to hone our strategic thinking and strengthen our friendships.

Somewhere along the line, as we maneuvered through these imaginary battlefields, I began seeing Alex differently. By seventh grade, I had a crush. Of course, Alex's best friend asked my best friend if I wanted to "go with" him. I couldn't get the *yes* out fast enough! Alex and I became "a thing." We didn't go out on dates like in the movies, but we found joy in studying together and playing Risk. We were young and deeply in "like," cherishing the innocent beginnings of a teenage romance.

That's when my dad had a midlife crisis, decided to leave the national lab and announced that he was moving us all to Houston. The news hit me hard. It would tear me away from my first real crush and the only town I'd ever known. Gah!

After we moved in the middle of seventh grade, I felt fractured and out of place and took six months to find my footing. I responded to the chaos by throwing myself into everything Texas had to offer—think academics and marching band—and slowly built a new life. But lightning does strike twice, and just as I was getting comfortable, another bomb dropped just two days before Christmas break: my parents had decided it was time to move again.

Coming of Age

At the ripe old age of 16, my parents moved me to California, where they had new jobs at the Lawrence Livermore National Laboratory. The one redeeming factor was that the trip included a detour through New Mexico, and I saw Alex again. He was beached on the couch after having his wisdom teeth out, but despite his puffy cheeks, I could see he had grown taller and more handsome. It was a brief but heartwarming reunion that I've never forgotten, though he doesn't remember it—he was hopped up on pain meds.

In California, I plunged myself once again into school, drama, speech and debate, graduating in 1989 as the valedictorian of my high school class and securing a spot at the University of California, Berkeley. The Berlin Wall fell that year, and it was a time of exhilaration for the world. It was also exhilarating for me, as I chose to major in politics and journalism to the shock of my science-minded parents. Dad was a nuclear physicist and Mom was a chemist, so they insisted I take science courses alongside my major—it was not a request. So, I became a political science major while also juggling physics, calculus, organic chemistry and physical chemistry.

At Cal, I did a gainer into the world of journalism and reported the radio news every evening. After two years, the relentless pace was making me rethink my decision to take so much on. Fortunately, it wouldn't be wasted time. Gradually, I found myself being drawn repeatedly to stories that combined health and science, seeing their potential to improve lives. It was a slow sunrise, but it eventually dawned on me that medical school might be my true calling—and I already had all the necessary prerequisites. Thanks, Mom and Dad.

Graduating from Cal in 1993 at the top of my class was a thrill, but better yet was reconnecting with Alex Brown. My parents had returned to Los Alamos, so I spent breaks there and visited him. Gone was the little pipsqueak who beat me at algebra—now, he was a tall, strapping guy who was fresh from Vanderbilt. Over plenty of tequila and beer, Alex and I realized that the seventh-grade spark was undeniably still there. He had grown up, and I liked the adult version. After graduation, we rekindled our relationship.

Adulting

In the fall of 1993, I began med school at the University of Chicago while Alex embarked on a master's program at Cambridge. Our paths diverged entirely, leaving us grappling with uncertainty about our relationship. It was rough.

At only 22, the thought of locking in my life partner was also daunting. It was intimidating. I wasn't ready. The timing felt off. Meanwhile, grad school was a lonely slog through endless library hours, and the distance and sporadic phone calls with Alex only exacerbated the loneliness. We were disconnected; I felt isolated and unsure about our future.

When year one of med school was over, I returned to Los Alamos for the summer, though Alex didn't return from Cambridge until late August. After he arrived, we spent six precious weeks together before he headed to Stanford for grad school, and I went back to Chicago for my second year.

When we were together, it was always the same—we were full of laughter and happiness. So, despite the fear and uncertainty, we committed to our relationship; perhaps sharing an unusual Los Alamos background and a relentless drive for success had brought us closer. Determined to make it work, we vowed to see each other every other month, scraping together money for budget airline tickets. We reunited every eight to 10 weeks despite the intense demands of our schools. The gate attendants knew us by name and smiled as we squeezed every possible moment out of our visits. It was a hard, thrilling time and we nurtured our affection, reserving one hour every night to talk and laugh together on the phone. We grew even closer.

Tragedy

When my second year of medical school ended, I eagerly headed home for spring break, fresh from my Physical Diagnosis class. This was the class where everything came together: disease states, patient history and the art of the physical exam. Eager to showcase my newfound skills, I decided to perform a physical exam on my mom. After asking her a series of questions and listening to her heart, I heard extra sounds that shouldn't have been there. She was just turning 52. I probed further: Did she get short of breath? Did her heart race sometimes? She nodded, attributing it to aging and menopause. I began to suspect she might have fluid on her heart. As my suspicions grew, I urged her with a mixture of pride and anxiety to get it checked.

Mom saw a real doctor who confirmed my suspicions with a serious diagnosis: she had an autoimmune disease similar to lupus that was causing fluid buildup around her heart. The medication she was prescribed was harsh, and it left her miserable. This was before advanced medications, so she had to endure high doses of steroids along with another drug to manage her heart swelling. New autoimmune symptoms kept emerging, making it clear this would be a long battle. While we were thankful for a timely diagnosis, we braced ourselves for the challenging road ahead, hoping for a sign of improvement.

I've always been proud of my mom. She was amazing, and her career was nothing short of extraordinary. Mom graduated at the top of her high school class and went on to study chemistry at City College in Queens, NYC, where she excelled again, graduating with honors. She earned her master's in chemistry at Columbia, where she met my dad at a party in 1962. They were married by 1964. Before having children, she endured several miscarriages. I wish I had known. Finally, in 1968, she had a baby girl, but at just six weeks old, she stopped eating, became listless and turned blue. Unbeknownst to anyone, she'd been born with a heart defect. My parents called 911, but the ambulance overheated while racing through the summer heat of New York City. Though my dad tried desperately to get it started again, my sister died right there in heavy traffic. My mom never talked to me about it; I didn't even know until my dad told me years later, when I became pregnant in 2003.

After her baby daughter died, my mom threw herself into her work. As a weapons chemist at Los Alamos, she was a force to be reckoned with in the WX-2 weapons chemistry division, handling classified projects she could never discuss. Her work

11

included investigating the Shroud of Turin, which she helped prove was not the cloth that had covered Jesus, earning her a mention in *National Geographic*. But her career's defining moment came when she began analyzing the USSR's chemical programs through satellite imagery and discovered a massive nuclear disaster in Khystym, high above the Arctic Circle, larger than Chernobyl. This discovery caught the attention of the CIA, who recruited her to work in counterintelligence. After aiding the CIA in several clandestine operations, she soon went on to join the CIA officially. In Houston, she collaborated closely with NASA. Later, at Livermore, California, she worked on additional secret projects, including one to encourage Soviet scientists to defect. The specifics of most of her work remain classified, and the most she would ever say about it was, "Some days are more exciting than others."

One Christmas break, we all went to a gun range to try out my brother's new .22. None of us expected to be great shots. I hit the edge of the target a few times, while my brother did a tiny bit better. Then, our dainty mom stepped up to hit dead center, shot after shot. We were flabbergasted! She just smirked, calling herself "an international woman of mystery." No kidding. Her career involved frequent trips to Washington, DC, where she regularly testified in closed sessions before Congress and the Intelligence Committee, briefing them on issues critical to national security. Although she couldn't share specifics, her work spoke volumes about her exceptional capabilities.

After leaving Congress one night, she called me feeling ill. I was deep into my third-year clinical rotations at the time and was familiar with the relentless demands of the emergency department. She described feeling terribly unwell, and as we reviewed her medications over the phone, my concern grew. I suspected she had dangerously high potassium levels and urged her to go to the emergency room. She was reluctant and just wanted to return to New Mexico. Still, I begged her to stop by the ER for blood work. Thankfully, she listened. They checked her blood and rushed her to the ICU, sharing my concern. Sure enough, a rare medication side effect had led her to critically high potassium levels and now kidney failure. The news marked the beginning of six agonizing weeks.

I flew home and dove into a whirlwind of medical jargon and dire updates to help my dad navigate the chaos. Mom was facing unforgiving complications and nothing we tried seemed to help; at one point, a necessary kidney biopsy nearly cost her life. Examining her kidney under the microscope, I was overwhelmed with disbelief and sorrow. Under heavy gloom, she stabilized just enough to leave the ICU, but her battle was far from over. Despite her doctors' best efforts, her condition continued to deteriorate.

At the same time, my brother's college graduation was approaching, and my mom pleaded me to leave her side and attend. Reluctantly, I left to witness my brother's proud moment at Duke, after which she insisted that I return to school. I had missed two weeks already, but I couldn't imagine tearing myself away from her. As she had told me about my science classes at Cal, for me, this was not up for discussion. After three days in Chicago came the 4 am call from my dad, shattering all remaining hope. My mom was experiencing uncontrollable seizures, a result of multiple strokes that had ravaged her brain. I flew home, knowing the end was near. Her speech was gone and her seizures were relentless. Soon, infection set in, and she became septic. Her doctor bluntly told me that we needed to write her a do-not-resuscitate order (DNR). Totally overwhelmed with anger and grief, I screamed at him before collapsing, overcome with pain as I realized the heartbreaking decisions that were upon me.

As reality set in, I made my mom the DNR, and her brother and sisters gathered as we moved her to comfort-based care. Mom was surrounded by family when we turned off the drips. She passed peacefully.

Something in me profoundly shifted after my mom died. My confident valedictorian facade crumbled, revealing a woman with a stark awareness of life's brevity. I was in agony, and it was the hardest time of my life.

My brother and I supported our dad for the following six weeks. Since I had to return to med school if I intended to finish, I went back to class a month and a half after Mom's death. Everything felt different.

My fourth year of med school began with an internship in the Boys Town neighborhood of Chicago on the AIDS floor during the height of the tragic 1996 AIDS epidemic. The hospital was filled with dying young men who were my own age, and there was very little anyone could do to help. It was hard, after sitting at my mom's bedside and turning off her drips, to be doing the same again day in and day out.

Before this, I had simply been a cavalier medical student who watched *ER* on Thursday nights because I was the same year as Carter. While I knew I didn't know *everything*, I thought that I was well on my way. Then, in '96, I realized I was insignificant. Twenty-four years of confidence evaporated over night and imposter syndrome flared to take its place. It began to feel appropriate, because as I sat with patients and bore witness to their final moments, there was no longer a cocky med student sitting beside them; she had vanished. In her place was someone who was simply honored to be trusted to offer them comfort.

Every morning, I'd drive to the hospital, pausing to watch the sunrise over Lake Michigan with Van Morrison's "Into the Mystic" soothing my soul while wishing I had someone to talk to about all this. If I had, I might've realized I didn't have to swallow my sadness and put on such a strong front.

Although I found purpose in my work, my mother's absence weighed heavily on me, and I began to worry that I hadn't helped her enough. I felt like it was my fault that she'd been diagnosed in the first place. It would take 30 years and a lot of therapy to put down the baggage of those questions…but in the summer of 1996, as a physician, I felt like a fraud.

Little by little, however, I began to realize that I was good at sitting at those bedsides as part of the final leg of each young man's journey. I was a witness, doctor, confessor and friend. It it was healing. Tragedy was everywhere, but we still tried to find the little bits of laughter where we could.

Being with my mom at the end and my experiences in Boys Town taught me to be a real doctor more than any class in medical school ever did. I learned to listen, care and realize that even if I couldn't cure someone, I could still do my best to make them feel better.

Future

The year was winding down when Alex and I got engaged during Christmas break 1995. Knowing what was coming, my mom and I had meticulously planned the wedding over the spring break before she died. It was bittersweet, but we were both aware of our limited time, and I knew I'd forever be grateful for it. Still, I had no idea that my mom had also planned an engagement party with Alex before he'd even asked me! I loved her for that, and we had a wonderful celebration.

I was finishing medical school, engaged and preparing for our wedding scheduled the week before graduation. It was also time to decide where I would do my residency, the next crucial step in my medical training. It was a marvelous time in my life—so much was happening! There was so much anticipation and celebration! Alongside my lingering sorrow and loss, there was so much joy, but I still missed my mom.

Alex and I were ready to be together, and for me, Stanford was ideal for blending a great internship program with proximity to Alex. Bingo. Alex's own PhD journey did seem endless, but because Stanford allowed us to live together in married student housing, it began to seem possible as we meshed our lives together. I had learned a lot about the fragility of life, so our happiness became the priority after a seriously brief, two-day honeymoon (marred by a bout of gastroenteritis, but let's not go there). Then, I plunged into my internship at Stanford University Hospital, with its grueling 3:30 am shifts which proved far less glamorous than their television portrayals.

Challenges

As my internship was wrapping up, Alex learned that his PhD thesis had been accepted and approved—three years earlier than expected! He excitedly considered job offers from various MBA programs across the country. While I was thrilled for him, I also felt adrift, contemplating what this new chapter might mean for us.

Finally, Alex accepted a faculty position at Vanderbilt's business school, as the "full circle" moment was too compelling for him to resist—he had completed his undergrad at Vanderbilt, so returning there seemed like a natural next step.

That meant our second year of marriage was to be spent apart—a harsh reality after four years of med school's back-and-forth. It was incredibly difficult, and the intense responsibility and unregulated hours of my second-year residency only made things harder, especially with the ever-present grief of losing my mom. Loneliness crept in as my days became a blur of hospital shifts and solitary homecomings—so different from the brief, happy life Alex and I had recently shared.

Residency was full of long nights wandering the hospital hallways on-call and waiting for my pager to go off. I had a patient named

Claudia, and we all knew she wouldn't leave the hospital. She was hilarious, smart and barely older than me, dying from leukemia after two failed bone marrow transplants.

With Alex in Nashville, I often sat with Claudia at night instead of going home to my empty apartment. We would talk until she fell asleep, and gradually we became friends. I even started visiting her on my nights off. There wasn't much for me at home besides houseplants and reruns of *Friends*. Despite very different lives, Claudia and I grew close, a bond forged in those quiet, late-night conversations.

One night, Claudia asked me why I spent so much time with her when I could be at home. I told her how Alex was across the country at Vanderbilt. She simply replied, "Why aren't you there, then?" Her question struck me to the core—I had never even considered it. I was so focused on staying on track to become chief resident and faculty that I hadn't stopped to think about whether that path truly made me happy. Claudia's simple question unmasked me.

I began to seriously consider it: What if I left Stanford for Vanderbilt? Residency transfers weren't exactly common—I had never heard of anyone doing it. What would I be giving up? And what could I gain? Claudia gave me the courage to ask myself these tough questions.

Two nights later, Claudia passed away peacefully in her sleep. The decision to leave Palo Alto was crystal clear after Claudia's death. What was I doing there? I was learning a lot, but I wasn't with the person I loved most in the world. I knew time was limited; Claudia had made that clear. Something had to change.

Mid-residency transfers are rare, and I knew it was a long shot, but I explained my reasons and held my ground. While my director couldn't allow a full transfer, they offered a compromise: I could complete elective rotations at Vanderbilt. Both Stanford and Vanderbilt were incredibly accommodating, and for that I will always be grateful. I spent most of the winter of my second residency year living and laughing with Alex in Nashville, returning to Palo Alto for core rotations. It was fantastic to be with him, and we worked on arrangements for my third-year transfer. It was a gift—one that Claudia's quiet courage had given me, allowing me to step off the carefully plotted path I had envisioned. At the end of that year, I left the Bay Area to join Alex and begin my new adventure in Nashville.

The third year of residency is tough; it's like boot camp, plus supervising interns and second-year residents. The timing was brutal. I had to hold my hat in my hand, make friends as I went and do the best medicine I could.

Alex and I bought a house, fenced in the yard and adopted a puppy. Though it was difficult being the new kid at work, I whispered a silent thank you to Claudia every day for showing me the way to find happiness in the moment—and when my mentor invited me to be a chief resident the following year, I was overjoyed. It had all been worth it.

Upheaval

At 28, I had weathered many storms and emerged stronger. Finally, my life seemed stable. Alex was teaching and I had committed to a chief year. We had a house and a dog, like proper adults. My career seemed promising. All the pieces were falling into place.

Just as the stars aligned, Alex admitted he was miserable teaching business students and couldn't see a future in it. He received an enticing job offer in San Francisco. I was angry. So much upheaval! It felt like I was constantly uprooting myself for him. Yet soon after considering the big picture, I realized I was keeping score—not helpful. Reflecting on what does and doesn't matter in life, I encouraged him to pursue happiness and acknowledged my profession's flexibility, allowing me to find work almost anywhere.

We arrived in California together, but I was uncertain, unemployed and deep in student loans. An ad in *The New England Journal of Medicine* caught my eye—a job opening at a hospital near Stanford, conveniently close to our new apartment. With only one functional car, the ability to bike to work felt like a sign. The universe seemed to be guiding me, offering a path forward amidst the confusion.

I dialed the number, landed an interview and soon worked under cardiologists caring for hospitalized patients. It was 2001, and this emerging field would soon be known as the Hospitalist Movement. My role involved close collaboration with the emergency department, overseeing patients needing overnight care.

The practice flourished. I introduced myself to numerous private doctors in the area, offering to care for their patients and leading to our swift success. The cardiologists were thrilled. I joined the board, which is how I got to know the hospital CEO, who eventually alerted me to the cardiologists' plan to sell the practice. I was furious! This practice was my baby, and the thought of it being sold felt like a betrayal.

Sequoia

The CEO and I brainstormed solutions and decided to partner with a group of emergency medicine doctors she knew. This partnership integrated my practice with a large physician group across California, providing the infrastructure we needed to grow. As Sequoia Hospital's Medical Director, I had the freedom to design a sensible work schedule and assemble a team of dedicated doctors. We decided to break away from traditional models, opting for a system that prioritized time away from the hospital. Partnering closely with the emergency department fostered a supportive and collaborative environment. Instead of the typical seven-days-on, seven-days-off model, we worked in four-day chunks with three days off in between. This approach proved more sustainable.

Alex was loving his new job, and I was flourishing in mine. We bought a new house and worked to pay off my medical school loans. Everything was going well, and our marriage was strong. We never saw what was coming next.

Heartache

Though thoroughly enjoying setting up a sustainable work model, I was also facing personal challenges. I was increasingly desperate to have children.

We had married young, so it seemed like we had all the time in the world. Alex and I joked that we should wait to start a family until we paid off most of our school loans. He didn't have any, Mr. Scholarship guy, but I had a bunch. Medical school is expensive.

We were already used to living off Alex's salary, so when I got my first paying job at 29, we used my salary to pay off the $250K in school loans. Finally, when we felt like we were close enough, it was time to get off the birth control.

All my friends were pregnant. I mean *all*. It was one baby shower after the next. I knew it would be my turn soon. Until it wasn't.

It wasn't that I couldn't get pregnant. I just couldn't stay that way. I lost the first two each at about 14 weeks. It was crushing; I could see them and hear the heartbeat, and then I'd wake up to cramps and blood everywhere. I had an extensive workup to see what was causing the trouble—nope. Nothing we could figure out.

Early on, I approached it like a scientist; the miscarriage happened due to a physiological cause. Then came miscarriages three and four. The baby showers got harder and harder to attend. I felt like I was in a parallel, dystopian universe.

The fifth time it happened was the worst. I was about 15 weeks and thought maybe we had finally made it. I was ecstatic...until the bleeding started. I had handled the others on my own, crying through the excruciating cramps, wearing the postpartum pads that I swiped from the hospital. This one, however, was too brutal; I couldn't make rounds at the hospital and got my partner to take my shift. I went home, curled in a ball in the shower with the blood swirling down the drain and thought I might never get up again.

Alex rushed home when I called crying incoherently. He scooped me up, helped me change and decided we needed to go to the movies. I'm not sure why, but he thought a change of venue would help. And buttered popcorn. And ice cream. Afterwards, we sat in the Mexican place next to the movie theater, eating guacamole. He just held my hand and said we were a team. No matter what happened, we would always be a team. I can't remember what the movie was, or how we got home. But I believed it would all end up okay.

Numbers six, seven and eight are a blur. I felt numb and angry but fortunately, not angry at Alex. I was pissed off at the universe, trying to keep my head above the waves. (I wish I had thought to get some therapy!) Just like my mom's silence about the loss of my baby sister, I felt like I was doing something wrong and never talked about it either. I soldiered on, trying to take care of my patients while holding all the broken pieces of my heart together.

I had eight miscarriages. Each time, I would reach 14 or 15 weeks and hear the heartbeat, only to lose the pregnancy. This agonizing cycle left me exhausted, empty and deeply saddened. Everyone around me was effortlessly having babies, and no one discussed the pain of miscarriage. Each loss produced deeper sorrow. It seemed interminable.

My OB is my dear friend, and her heart was breaking for me each time. She was at her wits' end, too. She suggested trying progesterone suppositories, thinking I might have a condition called luteal phase defect, where my body wasn't making enough progesterone during early pregnancy before the placenta takes over that job. I was willing to try anything. I had nothing to lose, so the minute two stripes showed up on the pregnancy test stick, I started shoving giant suppositories up my vagina.

They worked! We held our breath for all of week 14. Then week 15. By week 16, my doctor was feeling good about our progress; I was not about to stop with the ginormous suppositories. They became my talisman. By week 20, even though I knew I didn't need them, I didn't stop.

Being pregnant in a small community hospital turned into a shared celebration. Every morning, colleagues would greet me and my growing belly, affectionately nicknamed Will Brown. Whenever we had a tough day, friends and I would slap the ultrasound probe on and hang out with Will in utero—being a doctor has a few perks. We celebrated with numerous baby showers, and the excitement was palpable. My God, what a journey.

Motherhood

Knowing the first baby *never* comes early, I assured Alex he should fly to a special family event. Just after he boarded the plane, my contractions began. Will Brown decided to arrive almost two weeks early. My doula stayed by my side for three days, because Will was sunny side up, and Alex struggled to make it back. He lived out the plot of *Planes, Trains, and Automobiles,* but finally arrived. On June 27th, amidst a whirlwind, Will Brown was born. It was the best moment of our lives.

Outside my hospital room, we literally had to use a signup sheet for visitors eager to greet baby Will. After such a rocky road, I needed some personal time. Still, it was heartwarming seeing how my home and work lives seamlessly intertwined. It felt like Will was a part of the community at our cherished hospital—so much joy after a long struggle.

Even then, we weren't free of challenges. Will and I came home, but I grappled with postpartum depression. I didn't want to admit it. On the second or third day, overwhelmed and convinced I couldn't care for Will properly, I told Alex we needed to return him to the hospital. Alex took Will for a walk and called my girlfriend, who came over to support me.

It wasn't quick, but I gradually began to recover.

Being a new mom was tougher than anticipated. I went from busy days of meaningful work, chatting with colleagues, to being alone, staring at my baby and questioning every decision. For someone used to a structured, scientific approach, the uncertainty was daunting—overwhelming. Parenting books cluttered every surface as I desperately searched for answers. The absence of my mom was again palpable.

Observing the madness, Alex suggested we lock away the books and follow our instincts. That turned out to be the best advice I received. Months went by, and I made it. After surviving the newborn phase, I vowed to always check in on new moms, understanding firsthand how unseen they often felt. It wasn't wine and roses; it was relentless hard work.

I stayed home with Will for nearly six months. By then, I felt more competent and connected with other new moms, but the loneliness lingered. Reaching out for help wasn't easy for me, but motherhood demanded it. I had to step out of my comfort zone and ask for support, realizing that during desperate times, seeking help was crucial.

I joined a moms' group. We met at the playground, taking turns watching each other's kids while one of us napped. These women remain some of my closest friends today. Those days were tiring and strenuous, but another challenge was just beginning.

Returning to work with six-month-old Will was an entirely new obstacle. Childcare decisions consumed me. My job had unpredictable hours; I was on call frequently, needing to be within 15 minutes of the hospital. I needed a different option entirely.

It was evident that I would need to *create* a practice that suited my needs, so I hired other women with young children. Together, we designed a system that worked. I employed women with babies or toddlers looking for part-time work to maintain their skills, crafting convenient hours for them. I also benefited, as this allowed me to work a little less and fill the remaining gaps with similarly situated women who also wanted to be home for their families. It was my priority to feed Will dinner, bathe him and put him to bed. It meant everything to me. My colleagues had similar priorities, and we were a new tribe.

Managing work and family was a feat. Even when I was on call, I made sure to be home for bedtime. Living close to the hospital helped, and I had a solid rapport with the emergency department. Before heading home, I would check in with the ER and all the nurses' stations to ensure everything was under control. Then, I would dash home to handle what was most precious to me: Will's bath, breastfeeding, reading and singing. Everyone at the hospital respected my schedule; they were part of my team because I asked for their help.

Hank

This routine continued for two years until I got pregnant with Hank. He decided to arrive three and a half weeks early out of preemptive love for his older brother. I was still on the schedule at work. Having done this before, I was able to prepare; I'd learned a thing or two.

Determined not to cancel anything, I completed all my usual Monday meetings on the day Hank was born, then went out on maternity leave. He arrived quickly and was an easy baby.

Rearranging things was constant and necessary, but I was fortunate to have the flexibility I had painstakingly built.

From 2006 until 2013, I aimed to be home for dinner, even when on call. At home, the boys knew the drill; if I was on the phone with the hospital, I wasn't to be disturbed. There are countless funny stories about the mischief they got into during those calls—little banshees. Despite the chaos, life was as good as it could be.

I immersed myself in the hospital community, joining the foundation's board, chairing black-tie gala events and meeting key community members. We were known as Dr. Denise Brown & Alex in the society pages. No one was sure if Alex and I even shared a last name, but too much time had passed to ask. Alex was cool with the single-word name. He said that he felt like Cher or Bono.

I also worked at my boys' preschool every Tuesday, never trying to balance or separate work and home, but weaving together the things that mattered to me in real time.

Help

Long, frustrating days were standard, but I managed by giving each task the time it needed and asking for help. I had a fantastic nanny when Will and Hank were babies. She provided flexibility; I couldn't afford to stress about childcare if I got stuck at the hospital. As the boys grew older, I realized we didn't need such intensive help. A friend suggested using an au pair. When Hank turned two and was potty trained, my nanny helped me choose an au pair to join our family.

The au pair experience was transformative. The boys shared a bedroom while the au pair had her own room. The arrangement offered 40 hours of childcare a week, with allowance for date nights or emergencies. It was crucial that the au pair could be flexible if I got stuck at the hospital, and I made sure this was clear from the start. Our au pairs were like big sisters to the boys, taking them to school, picking them up and arranging playdates. After work, I took the boys to the park to have fun while the au pair made dinner. Alex's work had become increasingly intense with frequent trips to Asia, so if it wasn't for the au pair, I don't know how we would have kept all the plates spinning—even the non-negotiable ones.

With an au pair, I shifted away from big, dramatic family outings to simpler, more enjoyable activities. We played in the backyard on a slip-and-slide or rode bikes on the sidewalk. The au pairs made it easier to spend special time with the boys. Whenever possible, outsourcing became my strategy to help me effectively manage my life and career.

Family is dynamic. Careers are dynamic, too. Much has changed and continues to change, but these principles have guided me. Looking at the big picture, I'll say that life's trial, pain, joy and opportunity have shaped me in unexpected ways. Top-secret scientist parents taught me about navigating personal and professional responsibilities. This lesson carried me through rigorous schooling and a deep connection with Alex, as he became my life partner. Our journey together survived a long-distance relationship, intense education, career decisions and building a family supported by a network of friends, colleagues and caregivers.

Painful loss and awareness of the brevity of life made me determined to prioritize personal values at work and home, bringing satisfaction to my life while creating an environment that supports other women facing similar challenges. My career and dedication to my family haven't competed with each other; they have complemented each other, leading to a deeply satisfying life (so far).

Chapter One

THE FAIRY GOD DOCTOR PRESCRIBES SATISFACTION, NOT SUCCESS

D o you aspire to have a family? A high-powered job? Both? Life is not about choosing one over the other and it's not about balance. Despite the superwoman narrative of the '80s and '90s, we can't do everything at the same time. Most of the time, today's decisions will influence and pave the way for the future you envision.

In this book, we are in pursuit of success-satisfaction. We'll get real. We'll get practical. You need nitty-gritty strategies for balancing immediate gratification with long-term vision. We'll celebrate the small wins today, knowing they are the building blocks of our future success. I hope this book will redefine success to include both the joys of the present and the promises of the future, creating a holistic and enriching path to true fulfillment for you.

The Definition of Success?

I asked five friends the same question: What is success?

I bump into these friends at yoga, the office, my kids' school, the water cooler and even at the mailbox. Guess what? Every single one of them first declared they had no idea, and then they offered wildly different answers! Here we go:

Sumi, who I see at yoga, believes that success means having financial wealth. She's working hard for economic stability.

Emily is my neighbor, and the mom I chat with at school events. She thinks true success means balancing her personal life and professional achievements. She's all about finding balanced happiness in both areas.

Shane, the world's greatest UPS man, believes hard work and perseverance can lead anyone to success. He shows it everyday, finding joy in his job and in the dogs along his route.

Ben *knows* it takes a village. Ben is a friend from the office, and he is sure that no one achieves success alone. He tells how mentors, therapists and a high school friend network have helped him along the way.

Todd finds happiness within. He lives next door and is my thoughtful neighbor who thinks that true happiness comes from inside us (although this is opposite from what his parents taught him). Todd is about the power of positive thinking and following his inner star in search of joy.

Good grief—I wanted one simple answer!

Scanning the landscape of professional achievements and personal milestones, the concept of success often looms large, but it is sooo hard to grasp. Why is it so elusive?! We hear plenty of narratives about success at work, school and home, creating an illusion of a magical destination that, if pursued diligently, we might one day reach. But exactly who gets to define this success? Why do "they" dictate the parameters?

Two days ago, I was behind a Bronco for 80 minutes on the Loop 360 with a bumper sticker that read, "Success is a Journey." Really? Underlying messages about success often suggest an ultimate destination for which we must strive. Most of us are taught that success is on the horizon, out there, something we journey toward. We just gotta get there....

I don't think so.

Chasing Success or Embracing Satisfaction

I'm aiming for something different. Something better. Straining toward nebulous success does not line up with the satisfied, holistic and joyful life I advocate for in this book. I'm aiming for satisfaction—let's get there together. Modern success and deep satisfaction are not the same thing. Over many years, I have come to understand that true fulfillment does not arise from conventional success but from deep satisfaction. Pursue satisfaction like your life depends on it, but as *you* define it, rather than success as defined by the masses.

This book is about you, not me. However, I'll give you a 30-second backstory to illustrate what I mean. Indulge me:

I was the classic oldest daughter who embraced responsibility and drive. I was the high school valedictorian, then pursued undergraduate studies at Berkeley and graduated at the top of my class. Next, I raced straight off to medical school where I finished at the top of that class, too—Stanford for my residency in internal medicine, and Vanderbilt as a chief resident. I started a practice of hospital-based internists which grew into a thriving business. I joined the hospital board and contributed to healthcare in exciting ways. During this period, I also got married and started having kids. Oh, and my husband and children were also achievers.

Most people would label all that as successful. I feel so damn good about all this that I, too, might *think* it is the success that makes me happy.

It is not.

Here is what I've learned along the way: The true essence of my excitement, happiness and fulfillment has never been found in these achievements, but rather in the joy and satisfaction from doing what was meaningful to me. These include long games of kickball in the park, watching my children grow into independent individuals and witnessing the positive effects of courageous career choices. Profound satisfaction has come from doing the things that meant so much in my life—bathing the boys, sitting with patients in their final moments and going on dates with Alex. This internal definition of ever-evolving satisfaction, rather than an external measure of achievement, has become my true definition of success.

Philosopher Søren Kierkegaard captured this sentiment in a way that resonates with me: "Life must be lived forward but can only be understood backwards."[1] It is easy to feel overwhelmed when faced with significant decisions, such as whether to become a mother, get married, pursue further education, move in with a partner, pursue IVF or accept a new job. If we focus solely on external definitions of success, we may inadvertently limit ourselves and our potential for genuine fulfillment.

Time to ditch, "When I get my degree, I will be a success!"

Time to embrace, "As I figure out how to run a business, I feel satisfied!"

Time to ditch, "When I put my kid through private school, I will be a success!"

Time to embrace, "As I learn jujitsu alongside my daughter, I feel satisfied!"

Time to ditch, "When I get two million in my retirement, I will be a success!"

Time to embrace, "As I use my money to rescue doggies, which thrills me, I feel satisfied!"

Time to ditch, "When I _____, I will be a success!"

Time to embrace, "As I _____, I feel satisfied!"

Let's rethink this, my friends. Hop off the formulaic prescription for success. Pitch it. Grab for what makes you satisfied. You'll have to think hard for it. That's okay.

Imagine approaching life differently: Instead of striving for a future point where we declare ourselves successful, we embrace the present moment and find satisfaction in our ongoing journey. To start, I encourage you to make a list of your personal and professional goals. Then, for each goal, ask yourself, "Am I finding joy and satisfaction *in this moment* as I journey toward this goal?" This shift in perspective encourages us to weigh our choices based on internal satisfaction rather than external validation.

The Role of Internal Versus External Validation

In his book *Drive*, Daniel Pink shares the surprising truth about motivation.[2] His book offers tons of insights from his research and interviews with experts. He says external validation, which includes rewards like money, praise and status, often drives us to achieve goals set by societal standards. While these rewards can motivate us in the short term, they may not lead to lasting fulfillment. He goes on: "Greatness and nearsightedness are incompatible. Meaningful achievement depends on lifting one's sights and pushing toward the horizon." Of course, this means we have to understand our horizon and in which direction it lies. More on that soon.

On the other hand, internal validation is driven by intrinsic rewards such as personal growth, a sense of purpose and the joy of the activity itself. This means finding satisfaction in the process, not just the outcome. For instance, if you're an orthopedic surgeon, internal validation would be felt in the act of helping athletes get healthy and back on the field, regardless of whether your name is on their state championship trophy or you are named Best Surgeon in Greater Chicago. In your practice, you might add the habit of catching your patient-athletes' next game or match. Investing in your intrinsic motivators will lead to more satisfaction and sustained motivation. This is where we get happy. This is my reason for writing this book.

When we make satisfaction our priority, our focus shifts away from chasing external markers of success—job titles, salary, recognition and status. Instead, let's cultivate purpose and joy in our daily lives so they resonate with our values and passions, leading to a more integrated and fulfilling existence. You'll find yourself less stressed, more at ease with yourself and less concerned about others' views of you. It's a short-cut to giving zero f***s. It took me a while to get here, so I want to give you the inside scoop.

The Importance of Micro and Macro Success

Life is complex. As we navigate it all, we've got to recognize the dual dimensions of success-satisfaction: the macro and the micro.

Picture yourself at 85. You're sitting on your shady front porch in the rocking chair—your old doggie asleep at your feet. You're reflecting on your life. This retrospective view represents the macro level of success—a broad, overarching panoramic view of our achievements and legacy. It's the big picture of what you have accomplished over a lifetime.

America is a culture steeped in emphasis on macro success—the big, juicy significant milestones. Freedom, bootstraps, independence and hard work; the American dream has a lot to do with macro successes. These are things like high school graduation, getting married, landing a new job, buying a nice car, having a baby, your child graduating from college, paying off your house, becoming a grandmother or your retirement party. These hallmark moments are considered definitive markers of a successful life. Society conditions us to believe that these grand achievements pile up to ultimately create a life of fulfillment and meaning. Undoubtedly, these are good things, and we should work toward them. Macro goals help and direct us in a hundred ways. Let's keep them!

However, this focus on macro success can overshadow the importance of everyday victories. It's easy to overlook the small triumphs contributing to our overall satisfaction and well-being. Think of the individual bricks that form a great wall, the multitude of links that comprise a strong chain, the bazillion stitches that make up a cherished quilt or the countless strokes that create a gorgeous painting. We have to ask: Are we so fixated on the distant horizon that we miss the preciousness of each step along the way?

Consider the joy in the smaller moments: learning to create a spreadsheet, your baby sleeping through the night, changing the oil in your car by yourself, attending a parent-teacher conference, packing a healthy lunch from home, making time for a co-worker's house-warming party, going to the gym three times in one week, being present at the tee-ball game, finally learning to write a solid article or remembering your sister's birthday a week early. These seemingly minor achievements are the building blocks of our daily satisfaction and, ultimately, our long-term fulfillment.

In my own life, I have found profound joy in these micro-moments. I have loved the satisfaction of successfully managing a busy workday followed by delight in a spontaneous family dinner; these tiny victories enrich my daily experience so much. Though small, each micro-success contributes to what I value most and generates a sense of ongoing satisfaction. They pile up to create joy!

Finding Satisfaction in the Small Wins

There are a few strategies that help me practice and celebrate micro-successes—see if any of these resonate with you. Maybe think through some of this in a "Satisfaction Journal." While it is fresh in your mind, you can track your campaign for personal satisfaction.

- **Daily Reflection:** At the end of each day, take a few moments to reflect on your small victories. What made you smile today? What challenges did you overcome? I find that this takes two minutes with a handy notebook called The Standard Memorandum, but anything like it will do.

- **Celebrate Small Wins:** Create a habit of celebrating small achievements, whether through out-loud gratitude, a handwritten note or a tiny prize—DOTS gumdrops or a pretty cupcake are my favorites.

- **Set Micro Goals:** Break down the dream into smaller, manageable tasks and celebrate each step you complete.

- **Mindful Presence:** Practice being present in the moment, appreciating the small joys and triumphs as they occur. I sometimes coach myself for this before I get out of the car, knock on the door or pick up the phone.

The Now Builds the Later

Plan now. Instead of waiting for the next big promotion to feel successful, relish the moment when you solve a challenging problem at work or help a colleague. Instead of measuring parenting success by your child's academic achievements, decide to find joy in their laughter, curiosity or ability to tie their shoes. To make a change, we have to embrace and celebrate these micro successes. It's the now that builds the later! It's these moments that stack up to create your future. Each minute of triumph, no matter how small, contributes a brick, link, stitch or stroke to our broader lives. We cultivate a more holistic sense of accomplishment and joy by hugging the micro and macro perspectives together into one cohesive, satisfying whole.

Fight some parts of the now. In our quest for (outdated) success, the present moment dominates our attention—the now. We crave instant gratification, immediate results and the adrenaline that comes from quick wins. I get it. This inclination is natural; after all, who doesn't enjoy a little victory? However, the reality, particularly in motherhood, career and other long-term projects, is that the true impact of our efforts may only become evident much later—sometimes decades down the road. This sounds bonkers (at first).

While we might celebrate the big events and achievements with fireworks and engraved souvenirs, the cumulative effect of our small, daily actions often remains hidden until viewed through the rearview mirror of time. This realization shouldn't discourage us from seeking satisfaction in the moment. Quite the opposite; it encourages us to find joy in the everyday, knowing that today's satisfying efforts are *actually* building toward tomorrow's successes.

Even as we strive for future goals, we can't neglect to cultivate satisfaction in our hour-by-hour lives. We can maintain motivation and joy by appreciating the small wins and recognizing their significant contribution to our larger journey. This mindset helps us endure challenges, but also instills a sense of accomplishment and inspiration, knowing that these small wins are stepping stones to future rewards.

Parenting as a Case Study

When I set sail on my parenting journey, I defined success-satisfaction as raising independent children. My goal was to become obsolete as a parent, empowering my kids to navigate life confidently on their own. I made deliberate choices, often met with skepticism, to foster this independence from a young age.

For instance, I allowed my toddler boys to make a mess every morning as they learned to prepare their own breakfast. This decision was not without frustrations—spilled milk and scattered cereal were daily events. Yet, I persisted by placing a small pitcher of milk on the fridge's bottom shelf and storing unbreakable bowls and Cheerios in the bottom drawer. It wasn't long before they could feed themselves in the morning. These micro-level victories every morning, where my boys proudly made and ate their breakfast, were immensely satisfying.

Fast-forward 20 years, and the payoff is clear. What began as a messy morning ritual has evolved into shared brunches, with my boys delighting in preparing a wide array of breakfast dishes. And my sons and their friends still enjoy spending time with me! It makes my heart sing. This is the essence of long-term success—seeing the results of our early efforts blossom into meaningful, enduring relationships, happiness and skills.

Think of a long-term goal you are currently working towards. What small daily actions are you taking today that will contribute to this goal? How can you find joy in these actions?

It's not an easy fight. Back up for a sec and look over your shoulder. Coming out of college or grad school, we are in career-mode, believing that now is the only time that truly matters. This mindset is ingrained from an early age. We navigate the pressures of choosing a major, taking standardized tests and defining our future at merely 17 years of age. The societal message is clear: You must have it all figured out now, aiming to be at the top of your game in every aspect. This intense pressure can convince us that the present moment is paramount, overshadowing the importance of long-term planning. Balancing immediate gratification with long-term vision is a challenge many of us face, but with the right strategies, it's possible to find a middle ground that allows us to enjoy the present while also preparing for the future.

There are perils in overcommitting to now. An overemphasis on the present can jeopardize your future if you're not mindful of the long-term implications of your choices. It's essential to consider how today's decisions will shape our later years. Following the logic and asking yourself, "What will this decision look like for me down the line?" can help juxtapose immediate desires with future aspirations. This is a proactive approach to long-term planning to keep you responsible and in control of your future. Get specific.

- If I put off my engagement yet again, how might that affect my life at 30, 50 or 70?

- I have always dreamed of being a mom. If I freeze my eggs now, at 33, how will I achieve this life-long dream?

- Family is everything to me! I really want to raise my kids near my parents in Minneapolis because I want them to know their grandparents. Should I take the director position now in Houston? It is the next step in my career!

- I think I will use full-day daycare so I can be promoted sooner. Is this the best option for my kids? How do I know if that is the right path?

- I spend so much of my paycheck on takeout meals, half of which end up in the trash can because we hate leftovers. My mother made our meals from scratch, so as a mom, I constantly feel guilty. Is this the best way?

- Do I need to take that super intense job right now if it compromises my overall life objectives?

- What would my future look like if I took the job in Hong Kong?

As you skipper your life with the dual roles of working professional and mother, it's paramount to reflect on what you want your future to look like. Decide what you really want out of life. Get your ass back in that rocking chair and think hard about what you want to see when you look back at the end of your life. Go to the mountains for a long weekend to figure it out if you need to. Write it down. Get it on paper, with specifics. The fog will lift, and you will see your life with clarity. Taking the time now to contemplate what truly matters to you is vital.

In the early stages of our careers, particularly right out of college or grad school, there's an intense focus on work. We become hyperfocused on job performance, career trajectory and professional growth, often sidelining other aspects of life. Also, American business culture often equates success solely with professional achievements. However, work should be viewed as a component of success and satisfaction, not the defining element. Reframe success at work.

Work is *the* path to success-satisfaction.

Versus:

Work is *a* path to success-satisfaction.

Shifting from the definite article "the" to the indefinite article "a" when referring to work allows for a broader perspective. This linguistic shift reflects a mindset change, enabling us to see work as one part of a fulfilling life rather than the entirety of our identity.

The path → *a* path. Small change, big difference.

Make choices based on that "a". Adopting and internalizing this perspective is foundational when making difficult choices. By recognizing that work is just one aspect of a successful life, we can make more informed decisions that align with our overall life goals. This mindset ensures that we are not sacrificing long-term fulfillment for short-term gains, creating a more harmonious and satisfying journey. Soon, satisfaction becomes a lifestyle.

I aim to integrate this perspective into our daily lives and long-term planning. We'll get tactical on balancing immediate career demands with future aspirations to make sure each decision contributes to a fulfilling and well-rounded life. Together in this book, let's redefine the hell out of success to encompass immediate joys and long-term goals, creating a life rich in satisfaction, purpose and holistic achievement. Yep, that's it.

If you haven't read Christina Wallace's insightful work, *The Portfolio Life*, run![3] Put a bookmark right here, right now and go read it. I'll be here when you get back.

I've always viewed my life as a portfolio, but Wallace has literally written the book on it, so I won't reinvent the wheel. Please note that the following section is my internalization of Wallace's work—full credit!

The Portfolio Life is your guide to thriving in a whirlwind world where the only constant is change. Wallace is a human Venn diagram. She combines insights from her career spanning the arts, tech and business worlds to offer a survival kit for your professional life. Here's the lowdown:

1. Forget being labeled as "left-brained" or "right-brained"—that's outdated. Modern neuroscience says our brain hemispheres are more like a dynamic duo than feuding siblings.

2. Be your own backup plan! Life throws curveballs—pandemics, economic upheavals, you name it. Wallace's solution? A career *portfolio*—a mix of skills and side gigs that keeps options open and anxiety at bay.

3. Ditch the 110 percent myth. Instead of burning the candle at both ends, aim for 85 percent effort. It's the sweet spot that prevents burnout and leaves room for the unexpected.

4. Rest is for the *strong*. Rest is essential, not optional. Incorporating downtime isn't slacking; it's smart strategizing for longevity and health.

5. Your Life = Your Portfolio. Don't let your job title box you in. Build a life rich with interests, relationships and

46

adventures—because you're more than your business card.

I see Wallace's book as an edict for crafting a life filled with purpose, flexibility and joy, even as the world spins faster. Get *The Portfolio Life*. Seriously.

Integrating Life's Threads Into a Cohesive Whole

The portfolio concept played out for me when I visited the Plymouth Plantation, a living reenactment of a pilgrim village from early America. I saw a woman, bonnet and all, sitting at a gigantic wooden loom. She was weaving threads together to create what was becoming a lovely picture in blues and reds. Life is like that, composed of various elements—family, friends, multiple jobs and personal interests—all woven together. Each thread, whether simple or fancy, thick or thin, contributes to our lives' overall beauty and complexity. This is important: The significance of these different threads may shift over time, sometimes more purple, sometimes redder, reflecting our evolving priorities and circumstances.

Prioritize what matters most. A helpful exercise is to list the top 10 aspects of your life that matter most to you, then rank them in order of importance. Yep, I'll keep hammering the same nail! Of the 10, identify your top three essentials—the non-negotiables, the elements you cannot live without. As life progresses, things change and priorities may fluctuate. Given the 24 very finite hours in a day, striving to excel in all areas simultaneously will lead to burnout. Instead, consistently focus on the top three essentials while allowing flexibility with your remaining priorities. This fosters a healthier mindset for time management, and better yet, aligns your daily actions with your long-term goals. Remember, it's your life, your rules.

Next, manage the threads. I hope the real weavers of the world will forgive my ignorance! The lovely pilgrim reenactor explained something about how the warp and the weft alternate in weaving. Let's stay with the metaphor. Incorporate your interests and commitments—book clubs, graduate school, mommy-and-me swim class, cycling groups, learning communities, family time, social gatherings—into your tapestry. If these activities are integral to your identity, they deserve attention alongside professional responsibilities. Being flexible with the "non-essentials" can alleviate some of the pressure, granting you the freedom to manage your time more effectively. So, maybe after the non-negotiables are planned for, you make time for the cycling club and one graduate class. Next year, you might shift the focus. The warp and the weft. This strategy reduces stress, enhances satisfaction and ultimately leads to a more prosperous and well-rounded life.

I should mention that many things I'm describing are within your control. Yet, we all know that things happen that are outside of our control like health issues, accidents, parents who need sudden care or being laid off. The non-negotiables and the top 10 priorities change with time. Having systems for decision making will help guide you.

Technology works its way into every modern conversation because it has made all of the above so damn difficult. The advent of remote work and ubiquitous smartphones has blurred all boundaries. While it's convenient to work from anywhere, we often work all the time. The culture of constant busyness in America suggests that perpetual connectivity is synonymous with success, pressuring us to check emails and messages even during personal moments—at the hair salon, dinner table or while bathing our children—disregarding the thoughtful, intentional flex of the warp and the weft.

Resisting the allure of constant connectivity is challenging, but we have to do it. The fear that ignoring immediate demands might hinder future opportunities can create unnecessary stress. So, setting boundaries is essential, even in entry-level positions. Just as we establish boundaries with loved ones, we must also set limits with work. This is not balance reentering the scene; this is living out of our established priorities and values.

Later in this book, we will explore specific tactics to help you maintain strategic boundaries while allowing flexibility to focus on what truly matters. These strategies will empower you to look back from your porch one day, content with how seamlessly your career, motherhood and womanhood have evolved into a single, integrated life.

We only have one life to live. Get out your loom and start weaving a fabric rich in joy, purpose and fulfillment where every thread is valued, and every moment contributes to a satisfied whole.

Satisfaction Journal

What does success mean to you?

Reflect on how your definition of success aligns with or differs from the perspectives shared in this chapter. Are you currently chasing external success or finding internal satisfaction?

What small, everyday victories bring you joy?

Take a moment to think about the micro-successes in your life. How can you celebrate and cultivate these small wins to build towards long-term satisfaction?

Are your current goals motivated by external validation or internal fulfillment?

Identify one goal that is externally driven and one that is internally motivated. How can you shift your focus more towards internal satisfaction?

How can you embrace satisfaction in your present journey?

Think about one area of your life where you are focused on an end goal. How can you find joy in the process, not just the destination?

Chapter Two

THE FAIRY GOD DOCTOR PRESCRIBES...
NO BALANCE

The circus is bonkers. Fun, but bonkers. The crowd is buzzing because it is primarily kids, eyes fixated on the staggering feats being performed in one of the three rings. One of my favorite acts is the plate spinner. This isn't your typical juggler or acrobat; this is a *master* plate spinner, a true virtuoso of balance and timing. With a flourish, he begins spinning plates on poles, each one a whirl of color and motion. As more plates are added, the act becomes a breathtaking display of agility and focus. Just as the audience wonders how many plates can be kept spinning, one wobbles perilously, teetering on the brink of disaster. The performer lunges to rescue the faltering dish and sets it back in motion. Repeat. Search Eric Brenn's "Plate Spinning" on YouTube for a fantastic visual.

Yes, plate spinning is a thrilling, hilarious, nerve-wracking and exhausting performance—it's also a perfect metaphor for our lives. Each of us is that spinner, keeping the myriad demands of work, family, personal interests and unexpected challenges in motion. In this chapter, I want to expose the myth surrounding *balance.* Let's talk about your life—how you can identify which plates are worth spinning and how many to spin. Which ones can be safely set aside? How can you gracefully recover when one inevitably falls? And is *spinning* even the best method? Let's take a hard look at the dynamic and the value of life's spinning plates, with the goal of transforming the chaos into a satisfying performance of skilled and joyful artistry.

Managing Momentum

The quest for work-life balance is a popular theme in self-help books and blogs. Type "work-life balance" into any search engine, and you'll be bombarded with millions of results, each offering a unique roadmap to this seemingly magical destination. I think balance is the mythical kingdom nestled just south of the equally elusive "Land of Success."

What a load of crap.

My friend Danielle found this out in real time. She's the IT person in one of the hospitals where I worked. Everyone knew Danielle for her dedication and willingness to solve *all* our problems (and then some). She was also an active member of a book club, organized 5Ks and loved to coach her daughter's basketball team. To most people, Danielle appeared to be managing it all. Because we were friends, I knew that in reality, she was on the brink of burnout.

Once, after missing yet another basketball game due to a last-minute work commitment, Danielle realized she needed to change her approach. She felt like she was doing a crappy job, and I started talking to her about the concept of plate-spinning. Inspired, Danielle decided to reassess her commitments. She started by creating a "Hell No List" on her phone, identifying activities that drain her and don't bring any joy or fulfillment. I cheered her on.

Danielle began practicing saying "no" to additional work projects. She also stepped back from some *ACOTAR* activities, choosing to focus on her daughter, who was growing up fast. After about four months, I ran into her again; she looked and sounded different. Satisfied. The selective commitment brought her joy, avoided burnout and ensured she had time for what matters most—her daughter. Go Danielle!

The notion of balance is fundamentally flawed. The concept suggests a zero-sum game where focusing on one area inevitably leads to neglecting another. We discuss balancing work and life as separate entities, but they're not. There is no "work-life" and "life-life"—there's just life. And in real life, the idea of maintaining a perfect balance is as realistic as finding a unicorn in your backyard.

If we dropkick the cultural bias of achieving balance, what might that free us up to do instead? Pitch out the "scales of justice" balance model and lean into the plate spinner.

Instead of striving for an unattainable equilibrium, imagine a life something like our plate-spinning circus friend. This performer isn't just balancing; they are dynamically interacting with multiple plates—some large, some small, some ornate and some plain. Each plate requires attention and skill, and the act is not so much about keeping them perfectly balanced but keeping them all spinning. Some plates spin fast on the tip of a pole; others sit on a table and rotate slowly. The performer doesn't give equal time to each plate but knows precisely when to give a plate a quick spin to keep it moving. Occasionally, a plate wobbles, maybe even falls. It chips, but it's swiftly picked up, set right and spun anew. This is the reality of managing our multifaceted lives—not maintaining balance but managing momentum.

It's an average Thursday. You begin the morning juggling emails and making breakfast for your kids. Then, you rush to a meeting while planning a family outing in your head. Each task is a plate, some requiring more attention at different times, and like the circus guy, you learn when to focus on each aspect of your life.

This approach acknowledges that while not every plate can or should spin at the same speed, they all contribute to the show— your life. By *actively accepting* that some aspects of our lives will occasionally slow down, wobble or even fall, we free ourselves from the guilt and stress of seeking perfect balance. Instead, we can focus on keeping everything moving in harmony, however imperfect it may be.

We're hunting for satisfaction, so let's talk about how ditching the balance myth can liberate us. We all want to lead more fulfilled lives. We will look at real women who thrive, not by maintaining balance, but by maintaining the momentum of well-chosen plates. I'm talking about plates spun in determined and decided lengths of time—embracing some chaos and finding joy in the motion. We'll soon see that sometimes the most memorable performances do not come from flawless execution, but from the graceful recovery of a fall.

As I was writing this chapter, I was yapping about it to an administrative assistant at work while she was helping me with a paper jam. She said—actually, she ranted—"Denise, you are describing me! I'm 38 with two kids and I do nothing but plate spin—hundreds of plates, I think. Every day, I live out a circus, except I'm the clown and not the plate spinner because all my plates have long since crashed and burned. Early mornings, yoga, breakfast for my kids, work emails, team meetings, school runs, soccer practices on different fields, PTA, DoorDash dinners, baths and homework. Time for myself is a freaking joke. Yesterday, my daughter Mia spilled orange juice on the front of my dress *after* we were in the car. I don't even know how that is possible. Lucas forgot his soccer cleats but didn't say anything until we were in the car line at school. My stress skyrocketed, and I wasn't even at work yet. At night, we rarely have time to finish all their homework, and I haven't cooked in ages. It's chaos. The thing I hate most is I always feel guilty about how badly everything is going. Please finish that book and give me a copy!"

Choosing Which Ones to Spin

You don't need me to tell you that you can only keep so many plates spinning at once. In the circus of life, some plates—our *non-negotiables*—are the fancy, ornate ones spinning at the center of our performance. They are precious. Our priorities are the parts of our lives that hold the most value and demand our utmost attention. Surrounding these high-value plates are other plates, which are less critical but still part of our show. We can switch these out depending on our current circumstances and energy levels, allowing us to adjust our focus in real time.

Managing this ever-changing array of responsibilities isn't just about skill; it requires what can only be described as savage discipline. I learned something about savage discipline from my niece, Daphne. She loves to buy graphic tees with cute, soft-looking monsters on them and wears them with both her work skirts and her lawn-mowing shorts. Daphne has a rule: She must give one away whenever she buys a new one. The "one in, one out" fashion advice applies perfectly here. Suppose you continually add new plates without ever taking any away; the inevitable result is overload, leading to stress and potential failure. Such savageness requires knowing what you want (reference your Satisfaction Journal) and sticking to that. Psychologist Angela Duckworth labels this as grit, and says it well: "Grit is sticking with your future, day in, day out, not just for the week, not just for the month, but for years, and working really hard to make that future a reality."[4]

Adopting a "Just Say No" or Joy of Missing Out (JOMO) approach is also essential. This can apply to family activities, volunteer work, babysitting your cousin's kids, social media, networking on LinkedIn, neighborhood get-togethers, errands or taking on new roles at your job. It's about making conscious choices not to overcommit, ensuring you don't feel overwhelmed.

To implement this, start by defining what you *won't* do. Keep a "Hell No" running list—perhaps in a note app on your phone—to remind you of your limits. For instance, when my children were young and in preschool, I was managing a hectic schedule. I was super busy running a practice at the hospital. I was on call every third or fourth night, and I was t-i-r-e-d. At home, I felt pressure to be a super mom and was compelled to create lots of perfect family outings. I'd think I was a horrible mom if I didn't take them to the pumpkin patch, the petting zoo or the train museum. It was exhausting for everyone. They often left us drained rather than fulfilled. By skipping the big trips to the theme park and opting for simple bike rides or short walks to the park, we discovered those warm-fuzzy family feelings we'd been missing.

Inspired by this realization, my "Hell No" list grew. I stopped baking cookies, doing arts and crafts at home (that was what preschool was for) and limited playdates. I was willing to sign up for snacks only, no coaching. I learned to volunteer for the kids' activities in a way that I could still enjoy but didn't stress me out. I became pickier and pickier about which plates I was willing and able to spin. This led to earlier bedtimes, more snuggling, picture books and precious time spent building with LEGO bricks. As my boys grew, so did my list. I tried being a homeroom mom once and quickly added it to my permanent "Hell No" list for the future, learning to volunteer only for tasks that didn't overwhelm me.

There are only so many things that we can do. We owe it to ourselves to figure out what things we like to do and lean into those. Leave the rest of those plates behind, and don't feel guilty about it (there's a whole chapter on guilt later). Don't get sucked into spinning more plates.

This practice of selective commitment isn't just for your personal life; it also extends to our professional lives. At work, resist the pressure to volunteer for every project. If you decide to take on something new, be strategic about what current responsibility you might need to set aside to accommodate this new commitment. This proactive management helps avoid burnout and keeps you from reaching a crisis point.

Like exercising a muscle, the ability to say no and manage your commitments strengthens the more you use it. This might give you anxiety at first. (Okay, it will.) This discipline is not about restriction but about making empowered choices, allowing you to focus on spinning the plates that matter most. There are lots of things that require choosing. I like what Brené Brown says:

> *I want to be in the arena. I want to be brave*
> *with my life. And when we choose to dare*
> *greatly, we sign up to get our asses kicked.*
> *We can choose courage or comfort, but we*
> *can't have both. Not at the same time.*[5]

Let's explore how this selective approach not only reduces stress but enhances overall satisfaction, teaching us to be present and invested in the activities we truly value.

It's time to do some soul-searching with the Satisfaction Journal you started. At the end of this chapter, write down your non-negotiables. Identify the core elements of your life that are most important to you. Do these things shape the decisions you make daily?

It helps me to create a priority list—I live by this. I start by writing down all my current commitments and responsibilities. Next, rank them in order of importance and necessity to identify which plates you need to keep spinning and which you can set aside.

Once you know what to set aside, you practice saying no. Begin with small, low-stakes items. Turn down requests or invitations. This will help you build confidence in saying no when bigger, more demanding situations arise.

I even find it helpful to stare a mistake or two in the face. Think about a time when a plate fell on you. How did you handle it, and how did you feel? Learn from that. It hurts for a second, but it helps you in the future.

Plates Will Fall

Life is unpredictable; there is no smooth sailing just because you decide on this mindset. Things always go off the rails, usually at the most inopportune times. Accepting that plates will fall is a leap toward being a satisfied, grown-ass woman. Disruptions and unexpected events are guaranteed. They suck. Life, in many ways, is a masterclass in managing uncertainty. But change and uncertainty don't have to lead to a crisis. They require flexibility and a willingness to make choices.

This reminds me of my driving lessons with Uncle Bill—a sage if there ever was one. He taught me many things (despite being so portly that he struggled to squeeze into my Honda Accord), including how to drive on frozen roads. When your car is slipping on the ice and you feel out of control, the instinct is to panic and fight the direction of the skid. But the most effective response is to steer *into* it. This counterintuitive action aligns with the car's momentum, allowing you to regain traction and control. Similarly, when things in life start to go off the rails, flexibility and a willingness to adjust your course can turn potential disasters into opportunities for growth. Thanks, Uncle Bill.

Steer Into the Skid

If we give up the need to have total control all the time, we can let the skid take us places we might not go otherwise. If we accept or even expect that things won't always go as planned, we are open to more possibilities. The only way to manage uncertainty is to meet it with flexibility. Embrace the skid.

My friend Sandra embraced the skid when, at the peak of her career, her mother was diagnosed with Alzheimer's disease. Sandra was a senior marketing executive faced with a choice: continue her demanding job or step back to care for her mother. She chose to reduce her work hours and spend more time with her mom. During this very difficult period, she started a blog to share her experiences and tips on life as a caregiver. It gained a large following crazy quickly and helped a ton of other people. This new venture opened up opportunities for Sandra to consult on caregiving strategies for working professionals, turning a personal challenge into a new career path.

Another skid story is about Leo, my husband's friend. Leo was a tech entrepreneur, starting a company to develop a sophisticated new app for food delivery services. However, during the development phase, he realized the market was oversaturated and competitive. Leo had invested significant resources into his app. Still, market research showed that he was entering a crowded field with slim chances for standout success. Leo (a total rock star) steered into the skid. He pivoted his business model to focus on a niche market—providing technology solutions for restaurant food waste management. This shift set his company apart and addressed a growing need in the industry, leading to success and recognition for innovation in a space less traversed.

This approach to life's uncertainties requires flexibility—a readiness to make decisions on the fly and adjust our plans based on current realities. Just as steering into a skid might lead you down an unexpected path, so too can life's surprises take us to unforeseen destinations. Embracing it can transform potential crises into opportunities for innovation and personal growth.

All of this leads us toward satisfaction.

If this concept speaks to you, get a copy of Nassim Nicholas Taleb's *Antifragile: Things That Gain from Disorder.*[6] Taleb explores the idea that certain systems, including biological entities, economic systems and individual careers not only withstand chaos and stress but thrive and grow in these conditions. He introduces the term "antifragile" to describe an attribute of systems that benefit from shocks, volatility and disorder. *Antifragile* supports steering into the skid and managing life's uncertainties by promoting a mindset that values flexibility, continuous learning and the ability to adapt quickly. Taleb's idea that we should focus on becoming more adaptable and resilient rather than trying to predict and control every aspect of our lives aligns with the notion of spinning plates efficiently and responding effectively when they fall.

Moving forward, we'll grapple with cultivating this flexibility not as a fallback but as a fundamental approach to life. Meeting uncertainty with adaptability helps us manage crises and leads to a richer, more fulfilling life experience. We'll talk more about turning life's unpredictable moments into personal and professional development opportunities.

As we conclude this chapter on balance—or the total lack thereof—remember that the goal lies not in preventing every plate from falling, but in knowing how to select the right ones and how many to spin to maximize joy and satisfaction.

How many plates are you currently spinning? Are they the ones that bring you joy and fulfillment? Are there plates that cause unnecessary stress, which you might set aside or pass to someone else? And when a plate does fall, as it inevitably will, how can you approach the situation with a mindset that allows for growth and learning rather than frustration? Do you feel satisfied?

I hope this chapter will be a starting point for deeper contemplation about how you manage the complexities of your life. As you navigate your daily responsibilities and the unexpected challenges that arise, remember that the beauty of the performance lies not in the perfection of the spin but in the skill and resilience shown in keeping the show going.

Embrace the ongoing journey of balancing *your* plates, knowing that each adjustment, each recovery from a slip, adds depth and satisfaction to your life's performance. Keep spinning, keep adapting and let the dynamic dance of life unfold with all its unexpected twists and turns.

Consider how you might steer into the skid in your own life. When faced with unexpected challenges or changes, can you find opportunity within the crisis? Can you adjust your grip on the wheel of life, not with fear, but with anticipation of what new paths might open up?

The skids and spins of life, while challenging, are also what make the journey rich, rewarding and satisfying. Choose your plates carefully and enjoy the spin; then, steer boldly into the skid if one topples.

Satisfaction Journal

Which plates in your life feel essential, and which ones can you safely set aside?

Practical Step: Make a list of all the roles and commitments you're juggling. Identify your top three non-negotiables and consider which ones you can release or pass on to others.

How do you handle situations when a plate falls or a commitment doesn't go as planned?

Practical Step: Reflect on a recent time when a plate in your life fell. Write down how you responded and whether you viewed it as a failure or an opportunity for growth. What could you do differently next time?

Where can you practice the "Joy of Missing Out" (JOMO) in your life to reduce overcommitment?

Practical Step: Create a "Hell No" list for the areas in your life where you feel overstretched. Identify at least two things you can stop doing or say no to in the upcoming week.

How can you "steer into the skid" when life doesn't go according to plan?

Practical Step: Reflect on a challenging situation where things veered off course. Write down what you learned and how you can approach similar situations in the future with more flexibility and resilience.

Chapter Three

THE FAIRY GOD DOCTOR PRESCRIBES NONLINEAR WOMANHOOD

Should I? Shouldn't I?

I stared at my 28-year-old friend Daphne as she collapsed onto her couch, kicking off her heels with relief. She tapped her phone and pulled up some questions she had for me. Her mind buzzed with questions, insecurities and doubts, each one jostling for space in her exhausted brain. Should I? Or shouldn't I? The question loomed over her like a dark cloud.

Growing up, Daphne had absorbed the cultural expectations for young women like a sponge. It was an almost impossible checklist:

- Finish school.

- Get a great job you love.

- Find a partner.

- Move in together. Get married?

- Maybe buy a place.

- Have a killer career.

- Raise kids.

Somewhere in between, she was supposed to get a dog, a cat or at least some plants and attend all her friends' weddings and baby showers. Daphne had been dutifully ticking off these boxes, but now, she felt like she was running out of steam.

I'd call Daphne an overachiever; she'd done well in school, graduated with honors, snagged a job at a marketing firm that she liked most of the time and even managed to squeeze in some time for workouts. Yet, her career wasn't the glamorous dream she had imagined. Long hours and demanding clients left her feeling drained.

She met Jake during her last year of college. He was charming, funny and seemed to have his life together. Honestly, they are fantastic together! They moved in together two years ago, renting a nice apartment in the city.

Things were good, but the pressure to move forward was building. Her Instagram feed was a constant reminder of everyone else's milestones: engagement rings, promotions, wedding photos, ultrasounds and baby bumps. Daphne's best friend Emily was getting married in a month, so her weekends were booked solid with bridal showers and bachelorette parties. The constant celebrations of other people's life events made her question her own path. She loved Jake but wasn't sure if she was ready for marriage, much less a baby. The thought of adding more to her already full plate made her chest tighten with anxiety.

And then there was the dog. Or lack thereof. Daphne loves animals, but they hadn't taken the plunge between her work schedule and Jake's aversion to pet hair. She settled for a few potted plants on the deck, which she managed to keep alive (mostly). But she felt a pang of longing whenever she saw someone walking their dog in the park.

One evening, as she sat at yet another friend's baby shower, surrounded by pastel balloons and onesies, Daphne felt a wave of panic. The conversation buzzed about baby names and nursery decor, but she felt like she was in a different world. Should she be excited about these things? Should she be next in line?

At this point in the story, Jake comes in and joins the two of us, just as Daphne says, "I just feel like I'm supposed to have all this figured out by now. School, job, partner, house, baby. It's a never-ending list, and I'm falling behind."

I shrugged. "Who says you have to follow the list? You can do things your own way, at your own pace. It doesn't have to be so linear."

Jake responded, "Damn right."

I felt the words resonate with Jake, and they resonated with Daphne, but the pressure still remained. Societal expectations, internalized checklist and FOMO all weighed heavily on her.

The cultural norms for young women are almost impossible. Daphne's angst reminds me of the "panic years," a term used by Nell Frizzell in her book of the same name to describe the period in their late 20s and 30s when women face intense pressure and uncertainty about significant life decisions. She says:

> *The Panic Years are different for everyone,*
> *and yet, in some ways, they are the same.*
> *This is the time in your life when you feel as*
> *though your options are narrowing, your*
> *life path is being defined, and you are*
> *acutely aware of the passing of time.*[1]

This phase of life is about grappling with decisions around love, career, friendship, fertility and family, all while watching so many peers follow the traditional, linear path. A sense of urgency and confusion marks it—the proverbial ticking biological clock! *The Panic Years* is about "the flux," a phase between adolescence and midlife where women face big life choices and pressures: "It's the period during which you're making choices that will affect the rest of your life—where to live, what work to do, whether or not to have a baby."[7] These years are about the fear of running out of time to have children and establishing one's identity and stability in a world where traditional milestones are shifting. During this time, women often feel torn between professional ambitions and personal desires, leading to reevaluation of priorities and life goals. Frizzell describes this time as feeling like "women possessed," juggling these demands and feeling urgent pressure to make the right choices.[8]

I'm panicking just thinking about everything *we think* we should achieve by some mythical deadline. No wonder women are stressed out at worst, and ambivalent at best.

I'm the daughter of a proper second-wave feminist, so I grew up believing I could do anything. That confidence carried me through medical school and residency. But as I hit my own panic years, I started freaking out and feeling behind. My college friends, who hadn't spent eight extra years in school, were getting married and having babies. Meanwhile, I was swamped at the hospital, and my husband lived two time zones away. I wanted kids but was exhausted, drowning in school debt and barely managing to keep my betta fish alive. I felt overwhelmed. Behind. I couldn't possibly catch up.

Nonlinear Womanhood

When we think about our lives as a checklist, a set of boxes to tick, we cement our thinking in a linear way. But real life, when lived authentically, is more of a meander in the woods than a set of railroad tracks heading in a straight line to the horizon. Sometimes you might be on the path with many other sojourners, and sometimes you're sidetracked by a butterfly or two that flit off into the forest. Eventually, you might find your way back to the beaten path, or you might just find a new way. Joy can be lurking when you allow yourself the freedom to do a bit of wandering. In a world where women are pressured to follow a linear path toward success, this chapter challenges the myth of a perfect timeline; the point is to empower women to embrace this meandering journey that celebrates individual choice, resilience and the freedom to define womanhood on your own terms.

There's no best or perfect time to find a partner, buy a house, change jobs or have a kid, and there's definitely no one perfect way to become a mother. The only path that matters is yours, and hopefully, it's filled with intriguing side quests, trips and detours.

We have to stop compartmentalizing the important parts of ourselves—work, partners and even children. Instead, bring it all along for the ride! Only then can we pursue an often tiring but ultimately fulfilling journey.

You might recall from chapter one that as a second-year medical resident, living apart from my husband wasn't working for me, even if it seemed fine for him. I made an unconventional move and asked my residency advisor at Stanford to help me transfer to Vanderbilt. This sort of transfer doesn't usually happen, but I asked anyway. Everyone was incredibly supportive. I moved to Nashville to be with him, and we bought a house and got a dog. Phew, I thought, I'm catching back up...But no! "Catching up" is linear thinking, and I was on the brink of enjoying nonlinear womanhood.

Nonlinear Motherhood

I can't help you decide if you want to try to have a baby. There's an overwhelming number of things to think about: global warming, economic pressures and your biological clock—how I hate that phrase! Beyond those, there are also career ambitions, relationship stability and personal readiness. It's not just about wanting a child; it's about considering whether now is the right time or whether it will ever be. The decision is deeply personal and uniquely challenging, shaped by your circumstances, dreams and the unpredictability of life.

Having a child is one of the few irreversible choices in life. As a woman, it's frustrating to feel the societal pressures that imply you alone are solely in charge of birth control, reproduction and most of the child-rearing. It's a nerve-wracking, heart-wrenching, courageous leap that brings exhaustion, exhilaration and joy. The weight of this decision is immense, blending fears of losing freedom and career progress with dreams of family and motherhood. It's a complex, profoundly personal choice shaped by external expectations and internal desires.

If you know women in their 50s, 60s or 70s, ask them about their journeys—you'll be amazed. These women wrote the book on nonlinear womanhood. Many had kids early, sacrificing education and careers, only to return to school later and become incredible business owners and entrepreneurs.

Lynn's Story

My friend Lynn's story is literally one of the most f***** up stories I've ever heard. The events unfolded like a series of tragic events straight out of a novel.

Lynn grew up in a religiously conservative farming family in an isolated part of the country. She had a boyfriend, Thomas, but things were very pure and simple. Everyone in their small rural community smiled at them and assumed they would get married

71

and have a family right after college (if not before). Lynn and Thomas were in love.

Lynn was 17 and in her final year of high school when her mom died unexpectedly. The family was devastated and descended into chaos. Lynn was the youngest girl, and while her distraught family never intended it, she was left to deal with her grief alone. It was reasonable that she turned to Thomas for comfort, and they eventually decided to have sex. Once.

A couple months later, Lynn discovered that she was pregnant. As a teenage couple, she and Thomas were scared. They were afraid of what everyone would say. Seeing her distress, Thomas became her rock. He was steadfast and loving and promised they would face their future together. Thomas told her they would get married, have the baby and do all the things they had dreamed of, just a little bit sooner than they had planned. They agreed and decided to tell her grieving father together the coming weekend.

Two days later, Thomas was on his way to the farm. Lynn paced, anxiously watching by the window for him to arrive. He was late. Then later. Then the phone rang. Thomas had been in an accident on a two-lane farming road. They never knew what happened or what hit him. Only two things were certain: Thomas was dead at 18, and Lynn was now pregnant and alone.

The grief was excruciating. Somehow and somewhere amid the agony of losing the two people closest to her, she finally found the courage to tell her dad and Thomas' parents about the pregnancy. Against all odds, she finished high school and had her daughter shortly after graduation. College and all other life plans were on hold.

Lynn's story took a heartwarming turn, mainly due to the support and love of Thomas's parents. A year later, she was able to pursue her dream of higher education, studying business and computers as a student and mother. When her daughter turned six, Lynn graduated and embarked on a career in IT.

Eventually, she met a good man, fell in love, married and had two sons. Her resilience was steadfast, and all three of her children were standing next to her the day she opened her cybersecurity firm. Today, that firm is thriving and worth $100M+.

Looking back, Lynn is compassionate towards her 17-year-old, frightened farm girl self. Despite the overwhelming tragedies, shattered dreams and relentless pain, she emerged with three beautiful children, a cherished grandson and friends across the globe. Her story is a testament to resilience and perseverance, turning tragedy into triumph.

Lynn is a poster child for the nonlinear womanhood I advocate in this book. However, if linear thinking describes the "proper order of events," we should ask, "Proper order according to whom? Who determines the correct order for your life?" Seems like it should be you.

Should I Freeze My Eggs?

Getting pregnant is no joke. It is not a cakewalk.

After I finished my residency at Vanderbilt, I was excited to settle in Nashville with two dogs. Then, out of the blue, my husband decided he didn't like academics and wanted to head back to Silicon Valley. What!? I was 29 and hadn't even landed my first real job! But I figured I could job hunt in the Bay Area just as easily, so we moved back. After only living together for half of our five years of marriage, I definitely felt ready to put down roots.

I thought I knew exactly how it would play out. There's no more perfect parent than someone who doesn't have kids yet. It's easy to feel confident and sit in judgment when you're not the one in the hot seat. "When I have a baby, I'll only have a water birth." And it doesn't stop there: "When my kid is a tween, we won't allow phones." The hypothetical is easy. Getting (and staying) pregnant can feel like that, too. Seems linear: find a partner, get pregnant, have a baby and maybe do it again. It'll be a breeze— until it isn't.

What if you haven't found a partner you want to have a kid with? You're not alone if you are knee-deep in the panic years and worried about your eggs shriveling up. This is why so many women ask me: "Should I freeze my eggs?"

The pressure to decide can feel relentless. The ticking of the biological clock is a real thing, so we have to acknowledge it. Fighting it with egg-freezing might be a good, nonlinear action, but there are bigger questions at play here. I have a 23-year-old friend in New York City who asked me if she should freeze her eggs. Twenty-three! She allowed me to copy our text exchange into this book.

Alli and Denise's Texts

Alli: So, my mom wanted me to ask you a weird question.

Denise: Weird questions aren't a thing. You know me.

Alli: Umm, okay. Do you think I should freeze my eggs?

Denise: Wait, what? You're like 23! You're f****** with me, right?

Alli: Seriously, two people in my yoga class are talking about it. I don't want to derail my career, but *I know* I want kids someday.

Denise: You get that 23 is waaaaay too soon to be worried, right? No one even knows the effects of super long-term freezing. Where's the pressure from?

Alli: You know Mom has grandbabies on the brain.

Denise: Yeah, from your brother, who is 30! Yeesh! You just got to NY—go live a little.

Alli: That's if I get my break, which is pissing me off too. Patience is NOT one of my virtues.

Denise: It's not even been a year—focus on auditions, yoga teaching and having some fun. We can worry about all that other shit later.

Alli: Guess so, but it seems like a worry *now*.

Denise: You're not behind, even if you feel that way. Some shit can't be all planned out ahead.

Alli: Yeah, but you know I want to.

Denise: Ha! That's why you have old ladies like me to remind you—

Denise: LIFE DOESN'T WORK THAT WAY!

Why are we freaking out and trying so hard to plan ahead that this is even a thing? We're being pushed to make these monumental decisions way too early. Consider the emotional and financial costs, too. Egg freezing isn't cheap; and that's just the initial cost. There are storage fees, potential medical procedures and the emotional weight of future uncertainty.

And what about the long-term effects? We don't fully know what happens to eggs or fertilized embryos if they're kept frozen for over five years. There are many factors to weigh: the science, the costs and the personal stress.[ii]

This is intense societal pressure. I advise you to pause and consider what truly feels right for you rather than what you think you should do because of external expectations. It's okay to take your time, explore your options and make a decision that aligns with your values and circumstances. Remember, it's your journey, and there's no one-size-fits-all answer.

There are excellent studies on pregnancy viability and live births, but not many on the long-term health of IVF kids. While it's tough to prove causation, some trends point to associations with increased autism, ADHD and childhood leukemia in kids born from embryos frozen for more than six months. This lack of data should give us pause. My simplified take? Consider holding off on freezing eggs until at least 30. More work must be done to understand these risks, and taking time to make informed decisions is crucial. If you are wishing to have a child now, think about how that might be able to happen in your life. What can you move around? Intentionally postpone? Rearrange? Confidently choose what you value the most.

I avoided all things pregnancy-related until I was 31. I had a job I loved, and I was building a practice and paying off my medical school loans. Alex and I decided not to try for a kid until most of my loans were paid off so I could stay home with less financial pressure—it never occurred to us that Alex could've stayed home! Finally, after three years of working my ass off, I paid off most of the loans.

It was time.

When you finally decide it's time to have a baby, a few things seem to happen:

1. Pregnant women and babies appear everywhere. It's like when you're eyeing a specific car and suddenly see it on every road—moms and babies are suddenly omnipresent.

2. Sex can get weird, but not necessarily in a fun way. You've spent so much effort avoiding pregnancy that switching to "trying to make a baby" feels different. It's important to talk about this shift with your partner.

3. Some women get pregnant quickly. We call my friend Marianne "Fertile Myrtle." If she even *looks* at her husband, she gets pregnant. Many do not.

I didn't have much trouble getting pregnant, but staying pregnant was a different story. Between ages 31 and 33, I miscarried seven times, each around the 14-to-16-week mark. I'd hear a heartbeat loud and clear, only to be curled in a ball on the bathroom floor weeks later, crying and bleeding. Over and over. I began to resent pregnant women and babies—okay, I hated pregnant women and I hated babies. Still, they seemed to be everywhere, with constant baby showers to attend. I wanted to hide away in a cave and never come out. Clearly, there was something wrong with me. With each loss, I became increasingly desperate.

There are tons of stories just like mine, and so many of us struggle.

As Erica Berman, a fertility counselor, explains, women facing infertility often become consumed by the desire to conceive:

> It is the first thing they think about when they get up in the morning and the last thing they think about before they go to bed at night. They often have difficulty concentrating at work and difficulty relaxing and/or sleeping. They are often tearful and moody. They can experience intense jealousy and resentment towards

others who are pregnant or have children. Often, they withdraw socially to escape these unpleasant feelings. Women struggling with infertility sometimes lose pleasure and interest in the activities they once enjoyed and can start exhibiting symptoms of anxiety and depression.[9]

Nonlinear Motherhood and Working-Motherhood

Let's bring this nonlinear thinking into motherhood, too. There is still no "perfect timeline" for your motherhood. There is also no perfect family—remember all the pictures of a family of four with a mom, dad, older brother and younger sister? There is room for individual freedom. Think about what you value and then plan.

Whether it's the old-fashioned way, IVF, surrogacy or adoption, let's say you're having a baby. How exciting—and how scary. There's plenty of fun in the lead-up to the big arrival—baby showers and shopping for adorable baby stuff. People always say that everything changes, but until it happens, you have no idea just how true that is.

Your body, your friends, your work—everything shifts as you become a mother. And if you're not careful, it's easy to fall back into cultural patterns you may not even realize you're following. Your body will never be the same. Whether you carry a child yourself or not, you will never sleep deeply again. Studies show that even women in their 60s who are mothers have lighter sleep cycles than men and non-mothers. One ear is always listening.

Your friends will shift too—late nights out have new consequences. Kids wake up early no matter what time you went to bed. Before long, you'll adapt your activities and travel plans to fit your new life.

Work probably changes the most. Do you keep working, modify your role or pause altogether? There's no one right answer, though everyone will ask you about it as your due date approaches. Until you're actually living it, it's tough to know how you'll respond.

Alex and I faced a rollercoaster of emotions with our miscarriages. After so many losses, we started planning for me to take extended time off work if we ever carried a pregnancy to term. We saved every penny for our "new baby fund." You already know that the struggle eventually ended for us, and it ended in joy. I hope that is the case for you, too. Very sincerely.

Thanks to Dr. Julie and some gigantic progesterone suppositories, I carried Will to term. I knew I needed some time away after he was born. Postpartum depression didn't help, but after about four months, I got restless. At work, I was competent. I knew how to be a good doctor and make people feel better. But with a baby, I had no clue.

All my friends were at work, and I was home alone, waiting for naptime to end so I could get out of the house. I was tired, lonely and unsure of myself. I realized I needed to start planning my return to the hospital and meet new parents in the same boat.

Sometimes, being nonlinear is something you can plan for, and sometimes, it is reactive. Regular evaluation of values, goals and plans is important.

I started talking to new moms at the park. Anyone with a stroller, really. It felt desperate at first. There was one woman I'd met at prenatal yoga, but I had no idea how to find her again. She was smart and funny, someone I really clicked with. Imagine my delight when, one day at the park, I heard someone say, "Did you go to Blue Dolphin prenatal yoga?" It was her!

Marianne came crashing back into my life, and our friendship saved us both. We had both named our firstborn sons Will without ever discussing it. We struggled with the transition from confident, capable working women to new moms dealing with insecurity and loneliness. Having her next to me, nodding in agreement, made everything easier. Twenty years and several kids later, Marianne and I are still best friends. I can't imagine my life without her as a friend, confidante and sister.

We took different approaches to returning to work. I eased back into hospital shifts when Will was six months old, working mainly weekends so Alex could be home. Marianne had a traditional 9–5 role with a long commute. After six weeks, she realized she couldn't keep it up. She met with her manager and negotiated a work from home arrangement. This was a big deal in 2004. Eventually, when the hours crept up, she quit altogether. She made a confident choice based on what mattered most to her, and it made all the difference.

81

So, where does this leave you? Life's journey, especially as a woman, isn't a straight line but more of a winding path. It's perfectly okay to take detours and side quests that make your journey uniquely yours. Think about Daphne's story, my own experiences and your circumstances. It's clear there's no perfect time for anything—finding a partner, getting married, pursuing education, changing jobs or having kids. The only timeline that matters is your own. Embrace the flexibility and seek support when you need it. It's okay to wander off the beaten path. You might just find more joy and satisfaction along the way.

Satisfaction Journal

How does the traditional life "checklist" align (or not) with what you truly want?

Practical Step: Write down any part of the checklist that feels out of sync with your authentic goals. Reflect on one way you can redefine success for yourself, even if it means taking a different path.

What would embracing a nonlinear path look like for you?

Practical Step: Imagine your life unfolding without the usual sequence of events. Identify one goal or value that excites you, even if it doesn't fit conventional expectations. How might you pursue it?

Where do you feel pressure to "keep up," and how could you release it?

Practical Step: Think of an area where you feel like you're falling behind. Write down what living by your own timeline would look like here and identify one action you could take to align with it.

How can you build a support network to navigate your unique path?

Practical Step: Reach out to someone who inspires you in their life choices, whether a friend, family member or mentor. Reflect on how connecting with supportive people can help reinforce your path and values.

Chapter Four

THE FAIRY GOD DOCTOR PRESCRIBES CHOICES, DECISIONS AND CONCESSIONS

There Is No Balance, But There Are Choices

My granddad used to tell me a story about raccoons and their love for shiny things. He'd say that hunters could trap raccoons by placing a bright little trinket inside a jar. The raccoon would reach in, grab hold and be so captivated by their prize that they wouldn't let go, even if they got stuck. My grandfather would chuckle and say, "You know, that dumb raccoon could have its freedom if it would just choose to let go of what it doesn't need." I think of that sometimes when I feel like I'm holding onto commitments, roles or expectations that no longer serve me. How often am I the raccoon, refusing to release things I've outgrown?

Sometimes, finding satisfaction is as simple as choosing to let go. In a world that champions the myth of balance, true satisfaction lies not in spinning every plate but in making intentional choices, letting go of what doesn't serve us and embracing a fluid approach to life's priorities. Our freedom and growth often lie in the power to pivot and redefine success on our own terms.

In Chapter One, we introduced spinning plates as a metaphor for managing priorities. Getting your non-negotiable plates in motion will set you up for satisfaction. If you haven't yet identified your three most crucial plates (and your set of less important plates), this is the time. As a young woman starting a family and career, mine were family time, alone time and couple time with Alex.

Family time shifted as my kids grew. When they were younger, evenings together were simple but prioritized. As they grew up, family activities evolved, and we had to be more intentional about spending time together.

My personal quiet time was sacrosanct—at least 30 minutes daily. This allowed me to recharge through reading, meditating or simply sitting quietly. It was my mental sanctuary.

Couple time with Alex was non-negotiable. We aimed for two evenings a month just for us. Early on, we'd wait until the kids were asleep and have an intentional dinner in the kitchen. As they got older, we realized the importance of leaving the house. Our solution? A neighborhood babysitting co-op. Four families rotated babysitting duties, ensuring each couple got their much-needed date nights. This arrangement meant we enjoyed two date nights a month and alternated babysitting on weekends. It worked perfectly.

These three priorities—family time, alone time and couple time—didn't require an overwhelming number of hours. The evening routine happened daily, but my combined quiet time and couple time only tallied up to about eight hours a month. Keeping these priorities clear and consistent kept me from feeling overwhelmed.

Plate Number Four

My fourth plate, steadfast and ever-present, has always been work. There were stretches when the hospital consumed my every waking hour, threatening to smash my three highest-priority plates. During these limited times, my responsibilities to patients were paramount. However, I made it a point to plan around these intense periods, ensuring that other priorities didn't smash into smithereens. We have choices. It's crucial to identify which plates you're willing to spin at any given time and to set clear boundaries to manage them effectively.

The rhythm and management of my work (the *way* I spun that fourth plate) evolved as my family grew. When my children were very young, I prioritized being home for their bedtime routines. This meant tucking them in and then heading back to the hospital until the early hours of the morning. I worked a lot more weekends during this phase because my husband could be home with the kids. By the time they reached school age, my priorities had shifted; I worked more during the day, ensuring weekends were reserved for family adventures. This flexibility was possible because I sought out opportunities that allowed me to align my work with my top personal priorities. Pursuing adaptability is part of creating your own destiny, rather than letting life dictate your path.

Aside from my three core priorities, several other plates rotated in and out. Friendships were vital, providing a much-needed support network. I occasionally took on additional responsibilities at work, such as committees and foundation work, which were optional but fulfilling. School-related activities for my kids also featured prominently, from volunteering to teaching art classes. Exercise was another plate I tried to keep spinning, often by biking to work to stay active without taking up extra time. Lastly, although not a priority when the kids were little, my love for travel moved up the list as they grew older. These rotating plates added richness and variety to my life. They brought me joy and kept me well-rounded, but they were held lightly and could be rotated out of circulation when necessary.

The plates that matter to you might differ from mine. Figure them out! Establishing this framework allows you to manage your priorities effectively. Be sure that each critical aspect of your life gets the attention it deserves. This disciplined approach provides a sense of control, balance, confidence and joy, even amid the chaos.

Becoming Indistractable

One book that profoundly impacted my approach to time management is Nir Eyal's *Indistractable*.[10] His insights into concentrated time management are super valuable, especially in a world where screens constantly compete for our attention. Eyal's framework will teach you how to dedicate your time intentionally, allowing you to be fully present in whatever task you're engaged in instead of getting lost in the endless scroll of social media or news.

The magic computer in our pockets—our phone—poses the biggest challenge. It's so easy to get sucked into a rabbit hole of notifications and updates. Eyal's techniques are designed to help you resist these distractions and interact with technology in a more disciplined manner. By controlling how you spend your time, you end up having more of it.

I won't delve into every tool and technique Eyal recommends; his book is a treasure trove of strategies worth exploring, order it now! What I will say is that applying these principles helped me become more focused and present. I grew in my ability to engage fully in each activity, be it work, family time or personal hobbies.

Adopting Eyal's strategies doesn't mean you have to give up your digital life. Instead, it's about creating boundaries and being mindful of how you use your time. It's not about eliminating distractions entirely but managing them in a way so that they don't control you. This approach to time management is crucial for anyone looking to balance the various demands of modern life. Incorporating Eyal's principles into your daily routine can significantly enhance your productivity and overall satisfaction. By being more deliberate with your time, you can know, within reason, that each moment is spent meaningfully. It allows you to manage the momentum of your priorities with greater satisfaction.

Reality check. In a perfect world, we'd have a partner by our side, tons of resources and endless help, making it easy to keep the important stuff in motion. But let's face it, that's a bit of a fantasy. You and I need to accept reality and set clear boundaries about what we're willing to do and what we're not. Remember our discussion about discipline from Chapter One? It's back, and it means business. Choosing priorities, maintaining momentum and staying disciplined means being honest with ourselves about our limits and sticking to the priorities we set. Embrace the imperfections and adjust as needed without guilt or unrealistic expectations.

Making choices brings both freedom and fear—the fear of making the wrong one. But instead of viewing it as fear, think of it as freedom. Even if your first choice doesn't work out, you can always choose again. Most decisions are not irreversible. It's perfectly fine to change your mind. This mindset opens up possibilities rather than limiting them. Embrace the freedom in your choices, knowing you can navigate and adjust course as needed. There are very few irreparable things. It's okay to change your mind.

Christina's Story

Christina had a knack for turning dreams into reality. In sunny Southern California, she built her wedding planning business from the ground up, becoming the go-to planner for stunning galas. Her weekends were a whirlwind of bachelorette parties, rehearsal dinners and picture-perfect ceremonies. Christina thrived in this hectic environment, orchestrating every detail with true finesse.

Then she met Adam. They fell in love and got married. It wasn't long before Christina held their first child in her arms. The demands of wedding planning clashed with her new role as a mother. Late nights and weekends, which used to feel like joyous celebrations, now felt like a tug-of-war with her family life. She adored her child and cherished her time with Adam, but balancing it all was overwhelming.

One Thursday evening, as she prepared for another big wedding weekend, she looked at her baby sleeping peacefully and felt a pang of guilt. The spark she once felt for her work was sputtering out, replaced by a longing to be present with her family. Christina realized she needed to reevaluate her priorities. The business she had poured her heart into now felt like a burden. Maybe she was spinning the wrong plates.

An unexpected conversation with a friend opened a new door. Her friend mentioned a part-time executive assistant role that might offer Christina the flexibility she craved. Intrigued and desperate for change, she decided to explore this new path. It was a significant shift, but she approached it with the same passion she had for wedding planning.

In her new role, Christina found a balance she hadn't known was possible. She worked from home, allowing her to spend mornings with her son and keep her evenings and weekends free for family time. The skills she'd honed as a wedding planner translated seamlessly into her new position, where her organizational prowess and calm demeanor shone.

As Christina settled into this new chapter, she felt fulfilled. Satisfied. She hadn't abandoned her entrepreneurial spirit; she had simply redirected it. Her journey was a high decibel shoutout to the power of choice and the freedom to adapt. It's never too late to redefine what success looks like.

The Sunk Cost Fallacy

The sunk cost fallacy is that sneaky little voice that says, "You've put so much time, money and energy into this—you *have* to keep going." It's our brain convincing us that we can't back out of a project, relationship or commitment, even if it's no longer serving us.

But here's the truth: just because you've invested heavily doesn't mean you're obligated to keep going. Those past costs? They're gone. They can't be recovered. So instead of letting those sunk investments dictate your choices, imagine asking yourself, "What's actually best for me going forward?" That's where freedom is—learning to release what's no longer working without looking back.

Many women face this dilemma, feeling trapped by their previous commitments. That's the essence of the sunk cost fallacy. It's a well-known economic principle; people persist with endeavors solely due to the resources already spent, rather than projected future benefits. The fear of change often outweighs the desire to pivot. But recognizing this pitfall is crucial. Just because you've invested heavily in one path doesn't mean you can't choose a different, more fulfilling direction. Acknowledging the sunk cost fallacy can liberate you from feeling stuck, allowing you to make decisions based on your newly established priorities, current desires and future goals—not past investments.

Making significant life changes isn't as simple as suddenly feeling overwhelmed and pivoting. These decisions arise when your current path no longer aligns with your core priorities. You recognize that what you're doing no longer lines up with the plates you wish you were spinning. Acknowledging this misalignment can prompt a reevaluation of choices. Don't sink into the sunk cost fallacy.

Christina didn't sink. In that casual chat with a friend, she expressed her struggles and growing discontent with her career, which had once been her passion. Her friend mentioned a part-time executive assistant position, sparking the thought, "What if something could change?" That off-the-cuff comment made to a friend suddenly got her thinking. She felt she could step into this role with a clear vision, defined boundaries and the flexibility she desperately needed.

I know this story firsthand because I was the friend, and Christina became my executive assistant. She was articulate about her needs: morning time with her son and nights and weekends free for family. We set up a work-from-home arrangement for Christina long before it was the norm. She excelled, managing her tasks efficiently in concentrated spurts. This allowed her to have ample time for her family. She welcomed a daughter soon after and was able to care for her elderly father. Moving away from a full-time role allowed her to balance her career and personal life seamlessly, contributing to her family's finances and engaging in work she was passionate about.

Fast forward about eight years, and Christina found herself at another crossroads. Her kids were heading off to school, and she started to feel like she wasn't living up to her potential. Despite her talent and success, she felt an internal push to do more.

This time, Christina decided to pursue further education, taking online classes to earn a master's degree in healthcare administration. She took control of her destiny by balancing her role as my executive assistant and leading a team of other assistants. With her new degree in hand, she transitioned to running an online corporate education program for 8,000 employees. She is a perfect case study of a woman continuously evolving and thriving in her career.

Christina's journey was a series of conscious decisions. She made three significant choices: walking away from her thriving wedding planning business, embracing a part-time executive assistant role and stepping into a new career based on her acquired skills. Her evolution wasn't a series of concessions but deliberate choices reflecting her priorities and growth mindset.

Christina's story reinforces the idea that few things in life are irreversible. What may appear as concessions to outsiders are, in reality, strategic choices that allow you to prioritize what truly matters. Her metamorphosis was marked by conscious decisions, showing that very few things in life can't be undone or redone if we have the mindset to grow and evolve. At the moment, choices might look like concessions to outsiders, but if they allow you to do what matters most to you, they are not concessions at all. They are choices. Period.

Concessions: Navigating the Balance Between Yielding and Mutual Benefit

As we near the end of this chapter, it's time to address a dirty word many of us struggle with—concessions. The notion of giving something up, conceding or compromising usually carries a negative connotation. The dictionary defines a concession as: the act or an instance of conceding (as by granting something as a right, accepting something as true or acknowledging defeat), the admitting of a point claimed in argument, something done or agreed to usually grudgingly in order to reach an agreement or improve a situation.[11] All of this sounds like yielding or surrendering. But wait! It's also described as a compromise aimed at mutual benefit. We have to grasp the duality here because, at some point, we all need to make concessions.

Let's not view concessions as inherently harmful, as if giving something up is always a loss. Concessions aren't just about what you give up, but about what you gain in return. They're about finding a balance that benefits all involved, allowing you to maintain momentum and spinning the plates that matter most without sacrificing your well-being. My friend Daniela faced a possible concession and leaned into it for her own satisfaction.

Daniela was a powerhouse—a high-powered Ivy League lawyer who became the youngest partner at her prestigious New York City firm. She was proud of her accomplishments and rightfully so. Her career was on an unstoppable trajectory, with her eyes set on becoming the top rainmaker at her firm.

But then life happened. Daniela got married, and soon after, she added twins into her life. Suddenly, late nights at the office and client dinners that once thrilled her began to feel miserable. She missed her children. The thought of being away from them so often gnawed at her.

After some serious soul-searching, Daniela realized that she needed a change. She made the difficult decision to step away from her role as the firm's rainmaker—a role that had defined her career—and transitioned to the position of financial partner. This new role offered a more predictable schedule, fewer after-hours commitments and most importantly allowed her to be present for her family. To some, this might seem like a concession or a step back. But for Daniela, it was a powerful and courageous choice that provided mutual benefit and satisfaction for both her well-being and her family's.

It's tempting to want to do everything, to be everything to everyone. But the reality is that you can't. I learned this when my boys were small. I was passionate about the idea of my kids attending a co-op preschool. I wanted them to be in an environment emphasizing play, where they could be little kids digging in the dirt and getting messy. I found the perfect spot—

a parent-run, play-based co-op. My older son Will was enrolled in the Tuesday and Thursday morning classes.

But there was a catch. One of the school's requirements was that parents work once a week at the school. At the time, I was in the midst of building my medical practice; it seemed impossible to do both. But, instead of giving up on the co-op I *really* wanted, I made a choice to completely rearrange my schedule. Tuesday became my day away from work. This was one of my non-negotiables. I focused all my work commitments on the other six days of the week, allowing me to be fully present with my kids on Tuesdays. I packed that day with errands, chores and dinner prep for our dinner-share group, which we'll discuss in the following chapters.

This wasn't about doing it all—it was about choosing what mattered most at that moment. I conceded the idea of being able to work every day of the week; in return, I gained precious time with my children during their early years. Win.

We will make mistakes, and that is okay. No matter how carefully we plan, errors still happen. We'll make choices that don't pan out as we hoped. But here's the thing—mistakes are not the end of the world. They are opportunities to pick again, refine our choices and keep moving forward.

Remember Marianne? Marianne was an executive at Yahoo, juggling the demands of a high-powered job with the realities of motherhood. She realized she was missing out on her son's life while spending hours commuting up and down Route 101. So, Marianne made a choice and left her job to pursue part-time consulting. When that also became too much—let's face it, part-time is rarely part-time—she made another choice.

Marianne enrolled in a bakery school, pursuing a long-held passion for baking. She was incredibly talented and started a customized cake and cupcake business. It was a hit. She even bought an old USPS truck, fitted it out and started selling cupcakes at concerts and parks—this was before the food truck revolution. Her business took off, but it soon began consuming her life in much the same way her corporate job had.

Marianne made another choice. She shut down the business because it was taking too much time away from what truly mattered—her family. She pivoted once again, focusing on working with the educational foundation of her kids' school district. She spent the next 10 years there, gaining a deep understanding of what schools were looking for in college admissions. Eventually, she opened a college counseling business, which has since flourished.

If you'd asked Marianne years ago, as she sat in traffic commuting to Yahoo, she probably would have laughed her head off imagining herself as a college counselor. Her journey is about the power of making choices, learning from mistakes and remaining open to constant evolution.

The key takeaway is that life is not about rigidly sticking to one path. It's about making conscious choices that reflect your values and priorities at any given moment. You're not giving things up—you're choosing something else that offers mutual benefit. So, as you navigate your own journey, remember that it's okay to pivot, make new choices and keep growing. These are another set of keys that unlock the kind of satisfaction we are aiming for in this book.

As we wrap up this chapter, let's reiterate that life is a series of choices and concessions—some small, some life-alteringly massive. Balance is a myth! It is the conscious decisions based on thoughtfully established priorities that allow us to navigate our responsibilities and passions with satisfaction. Whether redefining what matters, as Christina did, or making what might seem like concessions, as in Daniela's story, recognize that these are not setbacks. They are strategic decisions that align with our evolving values and goals. Mistakes will happen, but each choice is an opportunity to pivot and grow. Life is less about perfection and more about progress, fueled by the freedom to choose repeatedly. So, embrace the journey. Establish and re-establish your priorities. Make choices. Make concessions. Keep your momentum and pursue satisfaction.

Satisfaction Journal

What are you holding onto that might be holding you back?

Practical Step: Think about an obligation, role or expectation you're struggling with. Write down what it is, why you hold onto it and the consequences of letting it go. Reflect on what freedom might come if you could release it.

Are your current priorities aligned with your vision for satisfaction?

Practical Step: List your top three priorities right now. Evaluate whether they align with what truly brings you fulfillment and joy. Identify one small adjustment you can make to bring them closer to your ideal.

How can you reframe your perspective on concessions and choices?

Practical Step: Reflect on a recent decision that felt like a compromise or concession. Write down what you gained from that choice and how it aligns with your values. Consider reframing it as a positive step forward.

Are there past investments that create a sense of "sunk cost" for you?

Practical Step: Identify one or two commitments that you're holding onto mainly because of past investments (like time and energy). Challenge yourself to consider if they still serve you. Reflect on how it would feel to release them or redefine them.

How comfortable are you with pivoting when your path no longer serves you?

Practical Step: Recall a time you made a change or shifted direction. Reflect on how it felt to pivot and the benefits that came from it. Write down a mantra or affirmation that reminds you that it's okay to make new choices that support your well-being.

Chapter Five

THE FAIRY GOD DOCTOR PRESCRIBES BOOTING THE TOXIC TRIANGLE OF COMPARISON, GUILT AND JUDGMENT

A t our sons' eighth-grade graduation, my fellow mom-friend Emily and I sat together, clapping as awards were handed out. One-by-one, kids were called to the stage for achievements in academics, sports, arts and leadership. I noticed Emily shift uncomfortably every time another name was announced. Her son Noah sat a few rows ahead, smiling and happily taking in the ceremony.

After another round of applause, a mom sitting in front of us turned and whispered to Emily, "I'm sure Noah will get one next year. He's such a good kid." Emily managed a polite smile, but I saw the hurt in her eyes. On the drive home, Noah chattered about his friends and his favorite part of the ceremony—when the music teacher tripped across the stage—blissfully unaware. Emily stayed quiet, her gaze distant. I could tell she was questioning herself, maybe wondering if she was doing enough. The load was invisible, but it was heavy.

Let's talk openly about the unseen weight we carry. As we switch up the many hats we wear and roles we play in life—daughter, parent, friend, partner, professional—there's an intangible weight that often accompanies us: the constant comparison to others, the guilt of not measuring up and the harsh judgment we place on ourselves and others. These feelings can be overwhelming, making us question our worth, our choices and our very identity.

Unseen forces and burdensome dynamics shape our lives, often in ways we don't even realize. With the pressures of parenting, the professional workload and the expectations we place on ourselves, comparison, guilt and judgment can erode our sense of joy and satisfaction. In this chapter, I hope to expose how comparison, guilt and judgment act as shrouded burdens that distort our sense of worth and rob us of joy. I want to explore how we can break free from these cycles to cultivate a life grounded in personal satisfaction, authentic relationships and self-acceptance.

You've probably felt the pressure of what I am talking about in a thousand situations like the one my friend and I experienced on her birthday. Sadie and I were lounging in the pool, our feet on the cool tiles underwater, the sun warm on our faces. It was her 36th birthday. Instead of feeling celebratory, she seemed lost in thought, almost defeated. I couldn't help but ask, "What is going on? Where are your famous margs? Why are we standing here in silence?"

She sighed, "I'm 36 already, and I should have done more."

I raised an eyebrow. "More what?"

She hesitated, clearly unsure. "I don't know...I just feel like there are things I should have done. Like, I should have accomplished more by now."

Her words hung in the air. I saw with my own eyes that this "should" was doing a number on her. Here she was—alive, loved, employed and surrounded by friends—yet that pesky "should" was stealing her joy.

That's when it hit me: "Should" is the gateway drug to comparison. It's the kind of word that drags you down into a spiral of feeling less-than. Who decided what she *should* have done by now? And why was she holding herself to some invisible, impossible standard? I hate seeing the weight of "should" on people that I love—and on women everywhere.

The Weight of Should

We've all been there, haven't we? Doom-scrolling social media, seeing those perfect snapshots of other people's lives—their glamorous vacations, perfect dinners, matching (clean) kids, their flawless homes—and suddenly feeling like we're falling short. But here's the thing: It's all an illusion, a highlight reel that leaves out the messy, imperfect reality of life. We all know that but fall prey anyway. The *should* is ingrained deep in our psyches. It is pressed down on us from childhood. Today, social media and digital media have added a million tons more pressure.

Teddy Roosevelt nailed it when he said, "Comparison is the thief of joy."[1] It's not just a catchy phrase; it's a vivid metaphor. When we measure ourselves against others, we are robbed of what truly matters—our own unique journey. Instead of appreciating our progress, we get caught up in what we haven't done, what we lack or how someone else seems to have it all together.

And let me tell you, comparison doesn't stop at stealing your joy. It invites guilt and competition to the party, too. The moment you start comparing, you're already behind, in a race you didn't sign up for. You're trapped in a cycle of "not enough," where you're constantly judging yourself—and often others—without even realizing it. Comparison, guilt and judgment are the life of the party in the worst way.

Guilt keeps reminding you of past mistakes, spinning stories about what you *should* have done differently. Judgment roams around the room, eyeing everyone critically, pinpointing flaws and making everyone feel out of place. And comparison is glued to its phone, flashing images of "perfect" lives and "better" parties and "greater" accomplishments, stirring that restless feeling of not quite measuring up. These three turn what should be a celebration into a night of second-guessing and unease. That was happening to Sadie, as it has happened to all of us.

Time to reclaim the party. Let's take a breath and let go of the "shoulds." They are not serving us. Instead, let's focus on our own paths, on finding joy in the journey and on being kind to ourselves. Because the truth is, there's no one way to live a fulfilling life. And that alone is something worth celebrating.

The Toxic Cycle of Comparison

Let's talk about the deadly whirlpool of comparison. When you start comparing your life, your work or even your parenting to others, you're setting yourself up for dissatisfaction. Parenting, in particular, becomes a pressure cooker when you let comparison creep in. Our modern lives are steeped in what I call "competitive anxiety." It's like there's this unspoken rule that loving your child more than the next mother means you must do everything flawlessly—whatever that means.

This anxiety isn't just a nagging thought; it's the fertile ground where parenting styles like "helicoptering" or "snowplowing" take root. These approaches, born out of anxiety and fear, often do more harm than good, despite our best intentions. They might originate from a place of love, but what's the result? We end up unintentionally stunting our children's growth and independence, treating them as if they can't handle life's challenges on their own.

Let's zero in on helicopter and snowplow parenting as an example, but you can apply this to lots of other things. Helicopter parenting revolves around constant hovering—always being there to pick up after your child, cut their food and even choose between ketchup or ranch. This over-involvement, though seemingly caring, teaches your child that they're incapable of making decisions on their own. Kids making small choices like these are crucial. That is how they build confidence and autonomy. When parents continuously make decisions for their children, they inadvertently communicate that their child's preferences and abilities aren't valued. This undermines the child's self-esteem and decision-making skills, leading to larger issues as they grow.

On the flip side, snowplow parenting is about preemptively clearing obstacles from your child's path, ensuring they never have to struggle. While it's natural to want to protect your child from hardship, this approach deprives them of essential life lessons. Challenges are not just unavoidable—they're necessary for growth. Without facing difficulties, children miss out on building resilience and problem-solving skills. This well-intentioned protection can leave them unprepared for real-world challenges, likely contributing to the rising mental health struggles among teenagers and young adults.

Ultimately, while these parenting styles stem from love and concern, they can stifle a child's ability to navigate life independently, leading to a fragile sense of self and an inability to cope with adversity. Here's what is true: we will all err on one side or the other with our parenting. Each of us is responsible for doing our very best to strike the right balance on this continuum, but we won't hit it perfectly, and no one else will either. It is good to read, research, learn and ask questions, but at the end of the day, you must choose the path that is best for your family. You can't be bogged down by the critical eyes of those who take a different route. Don't be that critical eye on them either; they are doing their best, too. Let's all take a flying leap off the comparison merry-go-round. It's not so merry.

These choices, along with decisions surrounding nutrition, sleep, education, discipline or extracurriculars, do matter. The effects of helicopter and snowplow parenting aren't confined to just raising children; they ripple out into our relationships and even our leadership styles. The tendency to micromanage—whether it's our children, our spouses or our employees—stems from the same root: comparison and the anxiety it breeds. When we constantly compare ourselves to others, we set the stage for judgment. We judge others for not meeting our standards, and we judge ourselves for not measuring up to some perceived ideal. This creates a toxic environment where competition replaces community, and instead of lifting each other up, we're all too often tearing each other down.

This behavior is particularly toxic in leadership. Just as children don't thrive when they're micromanaged by their parents, no one wants to be micromanaged by their boss. Yet we often feel compelled to do exactly that. The same anxieties that push us to hover over our children can push us to hover over our colleagues or partners, creating a stifling atmosphere that hinders growth and creativity.

In relationships, this can manifest as a helicopter partner or spouse—someone constantly nitpicking or trying to manage every aspect of their partner's life. Or it could show up as a snowplow spouse, who tries to smooth out every potential bump in the road before it even appears, unintentionally stripping their partner of the opportunity to handle challenges on their own. I've been dwelling on parenting here, but it is just as true in our personal and professional lives.

I remember talking about this on a walk with my friend Susie. She is a great person—conscientious, hard-working and kind. As we walked together, she opened up about something weighing on her.

She'd been passed over for a promotion at work, one she'd been working toward for years. The promotion had gone to a younger, newer coworker, and Susie had been blindsided. She admitted that she felt frustrated and even embarrassed, despite knowing how hard she'd worked.

"What makes it worse," she said, "is seeing how perfect her life looks outside of work, too. She's always posting photos of her morning yoga routines, her amazing outfits, her boyfriend who cooks nice dinners...I feel like I can't measure up and this proves it."

So, this wasn't just about the promotion—it was the spiral of comparing every part of her life to someone else's. Susie is one of the most dedicated people I know, managing work deadlines while being all-in raising her kids. Yet here she was, questioning herself and wondering if she measured up. She even admitted that she'd started to feel resentful, something so out of character for her.

After our walk, I thought about how universal Susie's feelings were. She had every reason to be proud of her hard work and her life, but comparison had stripped her of that pride, leaving her with a sense of "not enough." This reminds me of how deeply these feelings can infiltrate our minds—how comparison and judgment don't just creep in socially but can erode our confidence even in professional achievements.

In all these areas—parenting, relationships and leadership—the consequences of these pitfalls are clear. They foster dependency, diminish self-confidence and ultimately prevent the very people we care about from growing into their full potential. Comparison and judgment will keep stealing your joy and the joy of those you love until you break the cycle. The key is recognizing where your need to control or compare is coming from and consciously choosing a different approach—one that values satisfaction, self-acceptance, independence, embraces challenges and prioritizes community over competition.

Mommy Versus Mommy

I want to give special attention to one of the most dangerous and insidious forms of competition among women: mommy versus mommy. This stuff can be venomous. It's that sharp glance you catch at school drop-off when you haven't had time to put on makeup, or the critical whispers you hear when you let your kids ride their bikes to school—like I did when my sons were in fifth grade. I faced plenty of side-eye and unsolicited advice from other parents who believed I was being reckless. But I knew my kids were capable, and I trusted them to handle the responsibility.

This kind of judgment doesn't just hurt the person on the receiving end; it erodes the sense of community that should exist among mothers and parents. It's visible at school events, in the extravagance of competitive birthday parties and in the filtered perfection we present on social media. This constant need to compare and outdo one another creates a superficial dynamic where there are winners and losers—but the real loss is much deeper.

My friend Katy told me about the day she took her seven-year-old son, Jackson, to the park. Jackson was always on the move, darting around with mega energy and playing pretend. While they were there, Katy ran into her neighbor with her daughter—a calm, quiet girl sitting under a tree, happily drawing in a sketchbook.

They started chatting, but the conversation was tense. Katy's neighbor casually remarked, "I just think it's important for kids to develop focus early on. All that running around can make them too scattered, you know?" She said it with a smile, but the comment stung. Katy felt as though her neighbor was judging Jackson's natural energy and her choice to let him be himself.

On the drive home, Katy replayed the conversation in her mind. She started questioning herself, wondering if she'd failed Jackson by not steering him into calmer, more focused activities. That offhand comment from her neighbor left her feeling inadequate, like maybe her parenting approach was somehow lacking.

Later, she told me how hurt and confused she felt. "I know Jackson is his own person—he's happy and thriving. But one comment can still make you feel like you're doing it all wrong."

A pile up of those experiences made us both realize how painful mommy versus mommy judgment can be, even in casual conversations. It turned out okay in the end and affirmed for

Katy that her parenting wasn't wrong; it was just right for Jackson. However, it hurt to get there.

What we lose in this relentless competition is the strength of our relationships—both with our fellow parents and our children. Instead of fostering a supportive community where we lift each other up, we end up in a cycle of one-upmanship that serves no one. The judgment that pits one mother against another chips away at the solidarity that should bind us together, leaving us feeling more isolated and less confident in our choices.

I want to single out one more pitfall: the trap of self-judgment. Self-judgment is perhaps the most damaging of all. Motherhood is already a challenging and often lonely journey, filled with moments of tedium and uncertainty. But when we internalize the competition and judgment we see around us, it becomes a destructive force that erodes our self-worth. The more we compare ourselves to others, the more we spiral into a cycle of guilt and dissatisfaction, leaving us feeling like we're never enough.

This negative cycle is incredibly hard to break. It leads to a deep sense of resentment—not just towards others, but towards ourselves. We start to believe that we're failing, that we're not measuring up and that everyone else is somehow doing it better. This is bullshit.

The only way to escape this cycle is to break what I call the "toxic triangle"—comparison, guilt and judgment. Let's be real, breaking free from this isn't easy. It takes a lot of courage to step out of this cycle, and even then, courage alone might not be enough. What you really need is a partner, collaborator, comrade or ally—a like-minded friend, a fellow mom or even a supportive teacher. This person can help you reject the constant pressure to compare, to document every moment on social media or to throw those Pinterest-perfect birthday parties. They can remind you of what truly matters and encourage you to focus on that instead.

For me, that "partner-in-crime" mom friend was Marianne. We decided together that we would go our own way—not the competitive, Monday-afternoon-playgroup way where the moms and kids spent their time one-upping each other. Nope. We had our own sit-happy-in-the-mud parties; we let our kids ride their bikes to school and make their own choices whenever they could. Sure, the outfits they chose for themselves were weird. The haircuts were strange, too—purple mohawks for everyone! Yet, our collective five kids grew confident in themselves in the knowledge they were capable and loved.

Finding someone who supports you in rejecting constant comparison is finding a lifeline. Together, you can resist the societal pressures that tell you you're not enough and instead build a life grounded in your own values and desires, not those imposed by others.

Choosing Satisfaction Over Isolation

When you start embracing your own path—whether it's allowing your kids to have simple, unstructured fun without worrying about everything being picture-perfect or choosing to invest in meaningful relationships over superficial competition—you uncover a deeper sense of satisfaction. It's in these moments that the real joy of life begins: being present, creating genuine memories and forming true connections with your children and your community. All (increasingly) free from the toxic triangle.

Choosing satisfaction over isolation means prioritizing what matters—those authentic, imperfect moments that can't be captured by a camera or measured against someone else's life. It's about letting go of the need to impress and instead embracing the beauty and authenticity of your unique journey. When you do this, you'll find that the sense of fulfillment and connection you've been longing for was always within reach, waiting for you to recognize its value.

There is hope. I hope you will make deliberate choices to break the toxic triangle. I want you to be courageous, reject societal pressures and seek out the support of like-minded individuals who encourage you to be your authentic selves.

Embrace your journey, imperfections and all. I know you'll not only find greater fulfillment but also create a more meaningful and joyful life for yourself and those around you. As you explore your relationship with comparison, guilt and judgment, consider these Satisfaction Journal prompts to help you realign with your true values.

Satisfaction Journal

How do comparison, guilt or judgment affect your daily mindset?

Practical Step: Identify one area of your life where you often compare yourself to others. Reflect on what triggers these comparisons and consider one small way to redirect your focus toward your own progress instead of others'.

What would it look like to let go of the word "should"?

Practical Step: Write down three "shoulds" you often tell yourself. Next to each one, replace it with a statement that honors where you truly are in your journey, without judgment.

Where do you feel judged or judge yourself most harshly, and how could you practice self-compassion?

Practical Step: Think of one recent instance where you felt critical of yourself or worried about others' opinions. Write a compassionate response to yourself that acknowledges the effort you're making and your unique strengths.

How can you start celebrating your own unique path, free from outside expectations?

Practical Step: Identify a recent accomplishment or quality that you're proud of, even if it seems small. Reflect on what it says about your values or strengths, and jot down one way you can celebrate or honor it as part of your journey.

Who can support you in resisting comparison and embracing your real self?

Practical Step: Think of someone in your life who values you for who you are, not for what you achieve. Make a plan to connect with them soon, even if it's just a text message or coffee chat. Reflect on how these interactions can help you stay grounded in what truly matters to you.

Chapter Six

THE FAIRY GOD DOCTOR PRESCRIBES REIMAGINED OUTSOURCING

Cedar Street Dinner Co-Op

Every night felt like a race against exhaustion: get home, wrangle the kids and somehow make dinner happen. For three of us on Cedar Street—Jenny, Steph and me—the daily scramble had become a shared battle. Steph lived two doors up, Jenny was just across the street and I was right in the middle. We each had two kids, all under six and we were exhausted, juggling careers, young kids and endless demands that stretched us thin. Then one evening, as the chaos of our toddlers swirled around us, someone voiced what we were all thinking: "What if dinner could just...show up?" That question would change everything.

It was a lightbulb moment. We could each take a night. One mom would cook for all three families, freeing the others from the hassle of meal prep. The idea of coming home to a hot meal without having to cook felt revolutionary.

So, we divided up the week: Jenny took Mondays, I claimed Tuesdays and Steph, along with her devotion to the Crockpot, took Wednesdays. That was it—three nights a week where dinner was handled. We didn't have to think about it, and more importantly, for two days, we didn't have to do it.

The beauty was in its simplicity. We bought identical Pyrex containers, filled them with four servings each and dropped them off at each other's doorsteps between 5:30 and 6 pm. No knocking, no chatting—unless we felt like it. You just opened the door, picked up your Pyrex and ate.

For six years, this was our routine. Jenny's Monday dinners were always reliable. On Tuesdays, I experimented. Then it was Steph's Crockpot Wednesdays. The food wasn't the most important thing—the relief was.

The Cedar Street Dinner Co-Op wasn't just a way to get dinner on the table—it was a lifeline. As working moms, we were constantly juggling too many things: jobs, kids, household duties and the endless to-do list that never seemed to shrink. We were physically and mentally tired, and the co-op became a way to take one thing off our plates—literally.

Why Resource-Sharing Matters

Resource-sharing isn't just about hiring help; it's about *finding or inventing help* in unexpected places. For us, it was a close-knit group of neighbors who became a community. We weren't just sharing meals; we were sharing the load. We didn't have to do everything ourselves, which made us better moms, partners and friends.

We've discussed priorities in previous chapters—spinning plates and deciding which ones you want to keep in the air. This dinner co-op? It was a way to focus on the plates that mattered, letting go of the ones that didn't. It freed up mental space, gave us time back with our families and, most importantly, kept us sane.

Let's face it—raising kids is a full-time job and then some. It drains every drop of your energy, patience and sometimes even emotional stability. You spend all day at work, come home to homework, housework, kid-questions, messes and tantrums. You're ready to collapse when dinner rolls around. The Cedar Street Co-Op was our solution to that daily grind.

Cooking had always been a chore for me—something I *had* to do, not something I enjoyed. My friends felt the same way. So instead of trying to be supermoms, we asked ourselves: *What if we didn't have to do it all?* It was a shift in thinking, an acceptance that we didn't have to do everything ourselves to be good moms. In fact, sharing the burden made us even better mothers because we weren't stretched so thin.

And the best part? It didn't cost us a dime. This kind of support swap is creative resource-sharing and doesn't require paying someone else to do the work. Sometimes, it just means pooling resources with those around you. For us, that meant Jenny, Steph and I became each other's backups. We cooked, we delivered, we ate—*and we survived.*

Beyond Dinner: The Babysitting Co-Op

Once we had dinner figured out, we realized there was another area where we were all struggling—getting a break from the chaos of parenting. Everyone wanted a few uninterrupted hours to themselves or with their spouse, but babysitters were pricey, and with six kids among us, the cost quickly added up.

So, we expanded our little co-op into babysitting. Each of us took one Friday night a month. That meant on one Friday, you'd have all six kids under your roof from 5:30 to 8 pm, but on the other two Fridays, you were free to do whatever you wanted—have date night, go grocery shopping or just sit in a quiet house for a few blissful hours.

It wasn't all smooth sailing—getting six kids between two and six years old through bath time was like herding cats. But we made games out of everything, and the kids looked forward to their "Friday Fun Night" as much as we looked forward to our night off. What started as a practical solution quickly became something more: a tradition. And when the kids were old enough, Friday night babysitting turned into sleepovers, flashlight tag in the yard and camping out on the trampoline under the stars.

For us moms, it meant we could recharge. The guilt of paying for a babysitter was gone, and we got time to breathe without being in mom mode. Just like with the dinners, we were all in it together. We trusted each other, relied on each other and made sure that we all got the break we needed.

Something surprising happened. Our co-op quickly became more than just a dinner and sitter swap—it became a cornerstone of our lives, something much bigger than any of us expected. Yes, we were sharing dinners and babysitting duties, but what we were really sharing was the weight of everyday life. We were each other's safety net.

Jenny's kids became my kids, and my kids knew they could always count on Steph. They say it takes a village to raise a child, and the Cedar Street Co-Op became that village. Beyond convenience, it gave us connection. We weren't just neighbors; we were allies in the trenches of motherhood. We supported each other in big and small ways. Whether it was covering for a missed dinner drop-off, taking an extra babysitting night or simply being there when one of us needed to vent about the endless pressures of being a working mom, we had each other's backs.

Over time, the boundaries between our families blurred in the best way. We shared so many milestones—the first days of school, birthday parties and lazy Sunday afternoons. Twenty years later, my kids still call Jenny "Mama Jenny," and she's as much a part of their childhood memories as I am. That's the beauty of creating a community—what starts as practical help can turn into something lasting and meaningful.

How Else Can You Share the Load?

The dinner and babysitting co-op worked so well because we all lived conveniently close to each other. But what if you don't have neighbors right next door? What other ways can you resource-share? We realized that resource-sharing could extend far beyond dinner with some creative thinking. It can for you, too. Brainstorm a list of your pain points and let your mind roam over the possibilities.

As our kids grew older, we expanded our community co-op into new frontiers. We pooled our strengths—Jenny was excellent at writing, my husband Alex was a math whiz and I could handle science. We became a tutoring team, helping each other's kids with the subjects we were best at. Our simple dinner co-op evolved into a collaborative effort to support our children's education.

You might not even realize the talents that lie within your neighborhood or social circle until you ask. There's always someone with a skill or expertise that can complement yours. Whether it's carpooling, tutoring, cleaning, cooking, driving, gardening, dog-walking, painting, music lessons, baking, gift wrapping, bookkeeping, elder care, house-sitting or swapping professional services, the concept of sharing the load is applicable in countless areas of life. If you dare to be the one who suggests it, you might be surprised at how many people jump onboard. Resource-sharing some of the responsibilities makes your life easier, but you also might create a deeper bond with those around you. You'll increase your satisfaction.

What If You *Do* Have Money?

Outsourcing can look a little different if you have extra room in your budget. If Instacart had existed, I would have happily paid for grocery delivery back when my kids were small. The convenience of having someone else handle the weekly food shop would have been worth every penny to avoid the hassle of dragging two kids up and down the grocery aisles.

When the kids got older and our co-op started to phase out, I found it was worth hiring a sitter once or twice a month so Alex and I could still enjoy our date nights. If you can afford to, outsourcing the tasks that drain your energy—like cleaning, tutoring or grocery shopping—can be a lifesaver. It's not about being lazy; it's about being strategic. The key to using your money wisely is to ask yourself: Where can this extra help make the biggest impact on my/our quality of life? Sometimes, it's worth paying for things that give you more time to focus on what truly matters. By spending money on tasks that free up your time, you get more quality moments with your family and yourself.

Childcare

Childcare, especially when you have a demanding job, is one of the most important things to figure out. So, I'll tell my childcare story—not as a recipe or prescription, but as an example to inspire you to find what works for you.

For some families, daycare works great. But with my unpredictable hours as a doctor, I couldn't rely on daycare. If my kids got sick, I had no backup plan, and as a doctor, calling out sick wasn't an option. When my boys were babies, I hired a nanny who worked from 8 am to 4 pm. If I was on call, Alex would take care of the kids.

Once the boys were a little older, we tried something different: an au pair. Bringing in an au pair turned out to be a perfect solution. I preferred au pairs from Germany, because their driving requirements are incredibly strict, and I felt confident in their ability to drive my kids around. This gave us flexibility, which is exactly what I needed. I had peace of mind knowing that the au pair could take care of the boys' activities, school runs and everything in between.

Our first au pair arrived when Hank was around two and a half. The boys shared one room, and the au pair had her own bedroom. The system gave us 40 hours of childcare weekly, which was a godsend. Having an au pair began as a practical decision, but we soon formed a meaningful relationship. That's the thing about outsourcing childcare—you're not just hiring help; you're bringing someone into your family dynamic. Trust is built over time, and that trust makes all the difference. We built trust with Nicole.

Childcare isn't one-size-fits-all. The au pair system was ideal for us. In my job, flexibility was non-negotiable. I needed to know that my au pair would be there no matter what on the nights I was on call. But outside of those critical times, I was happy for her to go out with friends and enjoy her free time. It offered me balance—trusting that she would be there when it counted and giving her the freedom to have her own life, too.

Nicole stayed with us for nearly six years. She started at just 19 and left at almost 25. She became more than just someone who watched my kids. She became a member of the family. By the time she moved on, my boys were independent, riding their bikes to school and no longer needing constant supervision. But Nicole had shaped those years in ways that went far beyond childcare.

Another parental stressor is the midweek childcare woes. One of the biggest frustrations for working parents is the midweek school schedule. I never understood why elementary schools let out early on Wednesdays—it's a logistical nightmare for parents who work. This is where sharing the load can save your sanity. If after-school programs aren't an option, hiring a sitter for those few extra hours on Wednesday afternoons can make all the difference. Maybe this is the pain point to share with a few other moms, so each of you handles one Wednesday per month. That extra help ensures your week isn't derailed by the early pick-up, giving you peace of mind and more time to focus on work or other responsibilities.

Let's be clear about one thing: resource-sharing and outsourcing does not mean passing tasks off to your partner. I cringe every time I hear someone say, "Oh, my husband is babysitting the kids tonight." No, he's not. He's parenting. This is a team effort. You're not outsourcing to your spouse; you're working together to handle the responsibilities of your household. We'll chat more about partnership dynamics, but for now, just remember— resource-sharing is about lightening the load from *outside* sources, not within your immediate family. Your partner is your teammate, not someone you delegate to. If partnership has nothing to do with outsourcing or resource-sharing, let's talk about what the Fairy God Doctor prescribes for *actual* partnership.

A Towel Story

Every Monday, Alex comes home and sees me folding laundry. He is awesome, so without fail, he grabs some towels and starts folding them. After 27 years of marriage, you'd think he'd know how to fold them correctly. Everyone on the planet knows that the only right way to fold a towel is in thirds. Nevertheless, every week, Alex folds them in quarters. This is a small thing, yet every time it happens, I feel my patience tested. Among the towels, I have to dig deep, stop and remind myself—*he's folding the towels!* In a partnership, it's not about having things done your way; it's about showing up.

The same goes for many tasks around the house. Whether it's laundry, dishes, pet training, loading the dishwasher, trash removal or breaking down the cardboard for recycling, the way things get done isn't always exactly how you'd prefer. But in a healthy partnership, it's way more important to appreciate the effort than to nag your partner about your preferences. If you're constantly correcting the details, you'll exhaust yourself—and your partner. Who has the time or energy for that? It tears down rather than builds up. In the big picture, a partnership is about more than just dividing chores and responsibilities. Partners support each other, share their mental load and appreciate the effort in achieving the result.

The Load

Earlier in this book, I declared that "There is no balance!" That is still true when discussing work-life. But in every personal relationship, whether it's marriage, partnership or co-parenting, the real challenge lies in finding balance—both in tasks and in emotional support. We all have a carrying capacity, and life becomes much easier when we understand how to share the load with our partners. Let's explore the importance of partnership, the mental load we carry and how we can foster better collaboration without keeping score or nitpicking the details.

Our everyday choices create a sum total: a load. There are different kinds of loads. One of them is the mental load, which is made heavier or lighter based on our choices—though choices themselves can be an exhausting part of the mental load. This is also called decision fatigue. You know that feeling when you've been making decisions all day—what to wear, what to feed the kids, which emails to respond to—and suddenly, the thought of making one more choice is enough to push you over the edge?

It hits when I ask Alex what he wants for dinner, and he says, "Whatever you want." I know he's trying to be considerate, but what he doesn't realize is that it's not the cooking that exhausts me—it's the deciding. All day at work I make decisions; it's part of my job as a doctor. So when I get home, even something as simple as picking a dinner recipe or take-out restaurant feels monumental. I just want someone to decide for me.

Decision fatigue is a real thing, especially when the mental load of running a household primarily falls on one person. The average adult makes over 35,000 decisions a day. For women, many of those decisions revolve around family life. It's mentally draining. So, when you're deciding what your kids will eat, when they'll sleep or where they'll go, it's not just a list of tasks; it's a constant drain on your cognitive resources. This, more than anything, is why dividing up responsibilities is crucial in a partnership.

When we were little, my brother and I sometimes stayed at our aunt's place. She had a lot of chickens, and we loved helping collect eggs from her chicken coop. One morning, my brother decided he could carry all the eggs himself—no help from me or a basket. Things started out okay, with him carefully stacking the eggs in his arms and trying to balance the enormous, delicate pile as he headed back to the house. He had a determined look, adjusting his steps to keep the eggs steady.

Everything was going well until he reached the porch. Out of the corner of his eye, he noticed a chicken had gotten loose because he didn't have an extra hand to shut the door. It darted from the coop like a rocket, startling him just enough to make him stumble. One egg slipped, then another, and the entire stack came tumbling down before he could catch his balance. Eggs cracked and splattered all over the steps while he stood there, wide-eyed and covered in yolk.

You can only carry so many things at once. Everyone has a carrying capacity—whether it's physical, mental or emotional—and the more you load into your own arms, the quicker you'll burn out and drop balls (or eggs).

Ask yourself some questions:

- What are you carrying right now?

- How much of it are you carrying?

- Why are you carrying it? Do you need to?

- What might you put down?

- What could you carry instead?

- How can outsourcing help you?

As women, we often take on far more than we can handle, trying to keep the eggs from dropping—work, family, kids and household responsibilities. If you are in a partnership, you can't, and shouldn't, try to carry everything alone. You have to consciously decide what's most important, how to share it and then let go of the rest. And this is where carrying capacity intersects with the need for communication and compromise in your relationship.

Keeping Score and Perfectionism

One of the quickest ways to create tension in any partnership is by keeping score. I've seen it time and again—couples who count how many times one person has taken out the trash or done the dishes. "I've changed the baby's diaper five times today, and you've only done it once!" Sound familiar?

Keeping score in a partnership turns everything into a negative competition. No one wins—everyone loses. You start to resent each other for tasks that really shouldn't matter. Sure, the towels folded in quarters bug me, but if I keep track of every time Alex folds them "wrong," I'll only drive myself crazy. In the end, he folded the towels, and that's what counts.

When we stop keeping score, we stop expecting everything to be 50/50 all the time. Some days, you'll carry more of the load; other days, your partner will step up. We aim to balance the load over time, not in every single moment.

There's an idea I love—embracing the "minimum viable effort." It doesn't mean you're slacking; it means you recognize that life isn't graded. It's not about pursuing perfection but about what gets the job done.

For example, Alex and I have agreed on who handles what in the household. He's in charge of paying the bills and taking out the trash, and I handle the grocery shopping and laundry. Is everything done perfectly? No. But it's done. The point isn't to nitpick or to demand perfection from each other—it's to joyfully get along in life with as little stress as possible.

Perfectionism, especially in household tasks, is overrated. What's the goal? To have a perfectly folded towel or to have a functioning, loving partnership? When you let go of micromanaging every detail, you free up mental space and encourage your partner to contribute. They'll usually rise to the occasion.

So, reject perfection and aim for something better: competence. It's easy to fall into the trap of helicopter parenting or nitpicking. But when you do that, you discourage your partner from even trying. Why should they bother when they know they'll be criticized?

In our home, we don't aim for perfection. Instead, we focus on doing our best. If Alex misses a spot on the dishes or folds the towels in quarters, that's okay. I don't want to create an environment with constant judgement. I trust him to get the job done.

This applies to parenting, too. Teach them new tasks and work *alongside* them until they are generally competent enough to empty all the small household trash cans, wipe the windows without streaks, unload the dishwasher, make a phone call, walk to the store or write a thank you note. Kids don't need to do everything perfectly; they need to see that it's okay to make mistakes and that effort is what counts. By focusing on competence and appreciating the effort, you create an environment where everyone feels encouraged to contribute.

Help Versus Partnership

Here's a piece of advice that changed the way I think about my marriage: Never ask your partner for help. I know that sounds counterintuitive, but the word "help" implies that the task is primarily yours, and that they're doing you a favor by assisting.

Instead, ask for partnership. You're in this together. It's about working together toward a common goal. Alex and I don't "help" each other around the house; we share the load. We've divided tasks based on our strengths and preferences, and we stick to them. The key is clear communication and respect.

When you ask for help, you're subconsciously reinforcing the idea that the responsibility rests on you alone. But when you ask for partnership, you acknowledge that it's both your jobs to manage the household and care for your family.

Complaining

Help and partnership are potent words. Words of complaint are also powerful, but in the wrong direction. It's so easy to fall into the habit of complaining about your partner, especially when you're venting with friends. But complaining, especially in front of others, can create negativity in your relationship that's hard to shake.

I love teasing Alex about the towels, but I only do it with a smile. Complaining about your partner without any lightheartedness only builds resentment. And once you start focusing on the things that irritate you, it's hard to stop. You begin to see only the 10 percent of your partner that drives you crazy, instead of the 90 percent that's wonderful.

Instead of focusing on the negatives, try finding the good. It's a far more interesting challenge to seek out the positives in your partner, and it will bring more joy to your relationship. Writing down a list of their strengths will do tremendous good.

Partnership is so much more than just dividing chores and responsibilities; it is also no less than that. Add to it intentionally supporting each other, sharing the mental load and appreciating the effort rather than the result. When you let go of control, stop keeping score and reject complaining, you create a healthier, more balanced relationship. Life's too short to obsess over laundry-folding techniques or who took out the trash. Focus on what matters, let the little things go and watch your satisfaction meter rise. Our lives will never be perfectly balanced, but when we stop keeping score and start focusing on working together, we create a more fulfilling, supportive relationship that can withstand the small imperfections.

On that note, let's circle back to outsourcing.

Accepting Imperfections

There's one thing about creative resourcing: It's never going to be perfect. When you resource-share or outsource tasks—whether it's childcare, cleaning or grocery shopping—you're handing over control. And that means things won't always be done precisely how you would do them.

When I had an au pair or used a cleaning service, they didn't always do things to my exact standards. Maybe they didn't load the dishwasher just right, or perhaps the grocery haul included green olives instead of black. But you know what? It got done, and that was what mattered.

Resource-sharing is primarily about freeing yourself from the mental load of those tasks. Learning to let go of those minor imperfections is liberating. After all, would I rather spend two hours doing my own grocery shopping and get the exact brand I want, or let someone else handle it so I can spend those two hours intentionally with my family? The answer is easy.

In every relationship—parenting, marriage or work—it's tempting just to do things yourself. It's often faster and more efficient, and you know it will be done the way you like it. But you can't do everything; trying to do so is hopping on the fast track to burnout. Outsourcing and resource-sharing is your way out of that trap. Sure, your teaspoons might end up with the soup spoons, or the kids' lunches have cookies instead of applesauce, but you'll gain so much more in return: time, mental space, energy and satisfaction.

Letting go of control is hard but necessary. You can't keep all the eggs from breaking by yourself, and you don't have to. Trusting others to help, whether through a dinner co-op, an au pair or a hired sitter allows you to focus on what truly matters. And if you end up with those green olives? Well, you can always pick them off.

Outsourcing and resource-sharing is more than just delegating tasks—it's about freeing yourself from unnecessary burdens. Sharing the load gives you the bandwidth to be present in your life. Letting go of the need for control is a form of self-care. Ultimately, it's all about prioritizing your time, energy and relationships and giving yourself the space to thrive. Remember, we are hunting for satisfaction here. Grab that journal and start imagining the possibilities.

Satisfaction Journal

What's your current carrying capacity? Are you nearing your limit?

Practical Step: List the areas in your life where you feel most stretched—physically, mentally or emotionally. Identify one small responsibility you could share, outsource or let go of entirely this week.

How do you and your partner divide the mental load?

Practical Step: Reflect on how decisions and responsibilities are divided in your household. Write down one way you could better communicate your needs or share the mental load to create a stronger partnership.

Where is perfectionism or scorekeeping holding you back?

Practical Step: Think of one task or responsibility where you find yourself nitpicking or keeping track of who does what. Write down one way to shift your mindset toward appreciation and effort instead of perfection or fairness.

How can you embrace collaboration in your community or household?

Practical Step: Identify one area where teamwork—whether with a partner, family or friends—could make a difference. Brainstorm a simple plan to collaborate or pool resources and take the first step to implement it.

What would trusting others more fully look like for you?

Practical Step: Reflect on an area where you struggle to let others take the reins. Write down one small, specific way to practice trusting their competence, even if the result isn't exactly how you would do it.

Chapter Seven

THE FAIRY GOD DOCTOR PRESCRIBES UBIQUITOUS SELF-CARE

When most people hear the word self-care, they think of indulgences like manicures, bubble baths or weekend spa getaways—luxurious but fleeting moments of pampering. But true self-care isn't a momentary indulgence meant to make you feel temporarily refreshed. It's the pursuit of satisfaction via a long-term commitment to your mental, emotional and physical well-being.

Self-care means being deeply in tune with your own needs and respecting them, whether that means taking a break, asking for partnership, saying "hell no" or setting boundaries. It's making deliberate choices that align with what brings you real satisfaction and letting go of societal presuppositions. Think about the many topics we've covered: linear pathways, mommy wars, curated Instagram lifestyles and the expectations we face from family, friends and even strangers. Self-care, in its truest form, is about saying, "I choose my own path, my own happiness, my own values."

I wrote about a time in my life when I thought I had to do everything perfectly—work, home, family. I was always saying "yes," pushing myself to the limit because that's what I thought success looked like. But there was no time left for me—my energy was completely depleted. I was confused and unhappy. I'm pretty sure those around me were, too. That's when I realized self-care isn't selfish. It's a necessity. You have to fill your own cup before you can pour it into others. I wanted to have rich relationships at home with Alex and my kids, with family, at work and in my community. I wanted to invest in them and us. The point of self-care is joyful satisfaction for you, with enough extra life to pour into others. It creates a positive cycle of fulfillment and connection that gives you more in return.

Here is a teeny tiny example. Once, after a day at the hospital, I found myself wedged between completing household chores or taking a moment for myself. I was exhausted but tempted to tackle the mess in the kitchen. Instead, I made a choice: I stepped outside, took a few deep breaths and let the quiet of the evening reset me. That simple act of pausing became a habit. It's my reminder that mental peace sometimes outweighs crossing another item off the list. I now live by a simple mantra: You matter. Your energy matters. Your satisfaction matters.

No one else is going to take care of that for you. Stop letting cultural ideals of motherhood or work define your worth. True self-care is about showing up for yourself first, then everyone else.

Kids don't care about clean counters or balloon arches. They care about how present you are with them. They want you happy, not burnt out, because when you are happy, you make them happy. And when they're happy, that makes you happy. That is the cycle we're striving for.

Before we turn toward the conclusion, I'm going to dip into the complex dynamics of self-care within relationships. This sounds like a balancing act, but I've already told you that work-life balance is a myth. You don't have to juggle it. You need to prioritize yourself, not just for your own sake but for the sake of your relationships—with your partner, your kids and everyone who depends on you. When you take care of yourself, everything else falls into place.

Lessons From a Poem: The Heart of Self-Care

One of the most valuable lessons I've learned about self-care didn't come from a self-help book or a wellness guru. It came from a simple poem that my boys' preschool teacher Mrs. Oxton shared with me. She was the kind of person who understood the value of connection. Her poem is a guiding light, a reminder of what truly matters when it comes to raising children and living a fulfilled life:

If I Had My Child to Raise Over Again[12]

If I had my child to raise all over again,
I'd finger-paint more, and point the finger less.
I'd do less correcting, and more connecting.
I'd take my eyes off my watch, and watch with my eyes.

I would care to know less, and know to care more.
I'd take more hikes and fly more kites.
I'd stop playing serious, and seriously play.
I'd run through more fields, and gaze at more stars.
I'd do more hugging, and less tugging.
I would be firm less often, and affirm much more.
I'd build self-esteem first, and the house later.
I'd teach less about the love of power,
And more about the power of love.
It matters not whether my child is big or small,
From this day forth, I'll cherish it all.

These words encapsulate everything I believe about self-care. It's not striving for perfection or meeting an impossible standard. It's being present, connecting deeply and giving yourself the grace to let go of the little things that don't matter in the long run.

I remember one hot and hazy afternoon when I was overwhelmed, trying to keep everything together—the house in order, dinner on the table, kids' activities all organized. That poem from Mrs. Oxton came to mind. I decided to stop, sit in the shade with my kids and draw with chalk. The joy on their faces reminded me that my time with them mattered *way* more than the to-do list. They didn't care about having the "perfect" mom; they just wanted one that was present and interested in the scribbles they were drawing. That moment cemented for me what true self-care looks like: letting go of my high standards in favor of connection.

Reading this poem shifted my perspective about my organized house and nutritious meals. It taught me that I could stop chasing the ideal and instead focus on the moments that bring real joy and meaning. It gave me permission to dropkick the frenzy.

This poem sounds like it is about regrets and woulda-coulda-shoulda. But it's about self-care, when self-care is defined as a long-term commitment to *your* mental, emotional and physical well-being. Self-care means creating space for those joyful moments—the LEGO-building, a long brunch, the kite-flying, hearing your dad's story one more time, star-gazing—where you're not just going through the motions but really living. Self-care is choosing connection over correction and love over control. Prioritizing self-care means finding the most satisfaction possible in life by making the choices that bring long-lasting joy. These choices don't just benefit you; they ripple out to your children, your partner and everyone else in your life.

The Partnership Priority: Who Comes First?

In relationships, especially in marriages or partnerships, we often grapple with the question: Who comes first—the kids or the partner? It's not an easy answer, and my take on it might be controversial, but it's rooted in long-term thinking. Your kids will be with you for 18 or so years, but your partner is likely there for much longer. In my eyes, prioritizing your partner isn't about loving your kids less; it's about ensuring the foundation of your family remains rock solid. Giving my best to my relationship with Alex was also doing my best at loving my kids and providing them with a safe and sturdy home life. A united, solid partnership is what allows you to be better parents. When you and your partner are in sync, you work together as a team to provide for and nurture your children. If the relationship weakens because it's always on the back burner, the whole family dynamic suffers. Prioritizing your partner doesn't mean you're neglecting your kids. Quite the opposite—it's about creating a strong, stable environment where your children feel secure. You also show them what a healthy relationship looks like, and that's a powerful lesson.

Inner Self-Care: The Emotional Side

Yes, physical self-care has its place—whether it's taking care of your body through exercise, eating well or even getting enough rest. We receive this message constantly from popular wellness culture. But the true foundation of self-care lies in the emotional space you create for yourself. It's the conversation you have when no one else is listening. What does that voice in your head say? Is it kind? Is it compassionate? Critical? Harsh? Pushing you to do more?

Inner self-care begins with learning to quiet that inner critic by stepping outside the societal pressures that tell you to be more—a better mother, a better employee, a better boss or a better partner. We've all internalized these pressures in one form or another. We often feel like we're failing if we don't have the museum home, Barbie body or fancy clothes for our kids. None of that really matters in the grand scheme of things.

One Friday in the fall, I was torn between staying late at work to finish some paperwork or attending my son's youth football game. The perfectionist in me wanted to finalize everything at work, but I decided to leave early. That night, watching my son make an important play, I felt an overwhelming sense of satisfaction—something no work accomplishment could ever give. I noticed the tiny cheerleaders, the moms and dads cheering and my son scanning the crowd for my face.

It's not the big, flashy moments that stick with you. It's not the titles or the awards. It's the quiet moments—the ones where your children, now grown, call just to chat. It's the feeling of being surrounded by a community that you've helped build. It's knowing that you've created an environment where people feel safe, seen and empowered to be themselves. Those are the moments that bring real, lasting satisfaction.

Be kind to yourself. You are not faultless. No one expects you to be, and they aren't either. Give yourself permission to let the mess pile up if it means spending an extra hour reading to your kids. Choose to laugh with your partner about the unfolded laundry instead of feeling like a failure for not getting it done.

Self-care, at its core, is giving yourself grace and recognizing that you are enough as you are. The world might not always give you that permission, but you can give it to yourself. And that's where real self-care begins—inside, with the way you treat yourself.

As we redefine self-care, remember that this personal investment doesn't just benefit you; it spills over into every area, including your professional life. Satisfaction at work often mirrors how well we care for ourselves—let's talk about why.

Self-Care: The Professional Connection

Success and self-care can be seen as opposites in today's hustle culture. We're taught that success comes from relentless work, constant productivity and an unyielding pursuit of more. But this model of success often leaves us burnt-out, disconnected and far from satisfied. So how does self-care fit into this framework of success-satisfaction? Surprisingly, it's *the* missing piece of the puzzle.

At work, I used to pride myself on being the go-to person for everything and everyone, the one everybody needed, always picking up the slack. I remember a particular project where I was completely cooked, staying late at the hospital night after night. One day, my team came to me and said, "You've been working too hard—let us handle it." I stared blankly. Really? Should I do that? What does that communicate to my team? I decided to let them handle it.

That experience helped me turn a corner. I realized that there was an arrogance about doing everything myself; I was denying others the chance to step up. It wasn't kind or in the best interest of my colleagues. Letting go and trusting my team not only allowed me to recharge but helped them thrive. They wanted to grow. Success doesn't come from being the end-all, be-all; satisfaction comes from building a supportive environment where others can also succeed—at work and at home.

It happened again a few months ago. I planned to host a family gathering while preparing for a major event at work. I thought I could balance both perfectly, but halfway through the week, I was

144

exhausted and irritable. Instead of continuing to chase the mythical balance, I had a frank conversation with my team, scaled back the family plans, outsourced a lot and let go of the need to do everything. Focusing on priorities over balance saved my energy and gave me peace.

We are all leaders in varying capacities, and leadership does not mean being the best and doing it all. In the workplace, self-care manifests as trusting your team and empowering them to do their best without micromanagement. By modeling self-care at work, you encourage those around you to take care of themselves, too. When your team is rested, fulfilled and not burning the candle at both ends, the quality of their work improves dramatically. You create a culture where success isn't measured just by outputs but by the well-being and happiness of the people involved.

When you prioritize self-care—whether emotional, mental or physical—you're not just caring for yourself; you're also enhancing your capacity to perform at your best professionally, and letting others do the same. Success doesn't come from working yourself into the ground. Satisfaction comes from working smart, from giving yourself the grace to slow down when necessary and from creating an environment that allows everyone—yourself, your colleagues and your family—to grow.

I'm not the first person to think this way, and I'm not making this up. You've probably heard of Paychex, the company known for its payroll and HR services.[13] They wanted to improve workplace culture, and they realized something simple but profound: People work better when they're rested. They encouraged employees to take sabbaticals—longer breaks to recharge, pursue passions or just step away for a bit.

What they found was remarkable. Employees returned with fresh ideas, more energy and a deeper appreciation for their roles. And it wasn't just the individuals who benefited—teams were more innovative, collaboration improved and overall morale soared. Paychex learned that rest isn't a luxury; it's a key ingredient in doing good work. It's a lesson in self-care: When you allow yourself time to breathe, you come back stronger.

Conclusion

Really, this entire book is about self-care, because finding satisfaction is caring for yourself, your life and those you love. So, I am going to review each of the previous concepts in this book and how they relate to self-care:

Self-Care + Chapter One = A Prescription for Satisfaction, Not Success:

Self-care embraces the shift from chasing success to pursuing satisfaction, teaching us to find joy not in distant milestones but in the daily actions and choices that align with our values. It's recognizing that true fulfillment isn't a future destination but a present commitment to our mental, emotional and physical well-being as we live out our evolving definition of success.

Self-Care + Chapter Two = A Prescription for *No* Balance:

Self-care lets us call out the myth of work-life balance for what it is—a clever distraction. Instead of walking a tightrope and trying not to fall, make intentional choices that let you focus on what truly satisfies you. Some things will wobble and others might crash, but self-care reminds us that life isn't about perfection; it's about prioritizing what fills you up, not what keeps you balanced.

Self-Care + Chapter Three = A Prescription for Nonlinear Womanhood:

Self-care means embracing the beautifully messy, nonlinear path of life. It's about giving yourself permission to take detours, change your mind and discover unexpected joys. Instead of stressing about staying on track, self-care encourages you to find satisfaction in the twists, turns and every moment in between, knowing that the journey is just as important as the destination.

Self-Care + Chapter Four = A Prescription for Choices, Decisions and Concessions:

Self-care means giving yourself the freedom to choose what truly serves your satisfaction and letting go of the rest—even if it feels uncomfortable. It's learning to release what you've outgrown, embracing the power to pivot and recognizing that every choice is an opportunity to align your life with your mental, emotional and physical well-being. Sometimes, self-care is as simple as unclenching your grip on what's weighing you down.

Self-Care + Chapter Five = A Prescription for Booting the Toxic Triangle of Comparison, Guilt and Judgment:

Self-care says to step out of the toxic triangle of comparison, guilt and judgment. It's choosing to focus on your own path, celebrating what satisfies you and letting go of the pressure to measure up to others. When you practice self-care, you replace self-criticism with self-compassion and find the freedom to thrive on your own terms.

Self-Care + Chapter Six = A Prescription for Reimagined Outsourcing and Partnership:

Self-care doesn't mean going it alone—it's about creating a community where shared responsibilities lighten the load. By leaning on your village and contributing to theirs, you cultivate mental, emotional and physical well-being, not just for yourself but for everyone involved. Self-care thrives in collaboration, reminding us that satisfaction grows stronger when it's shared. Self-care in a partnership is about sharing the load, not keeping score. It's recognizing that satisfaction grows when both partners work together—not perfectly, but thoughtfully. By letting go of control, rejecting perfectionism and embracing collaboration, self-care fosters a relationship built on mutual respect, understanding and appreciation for each other's contributions— whether the towels are folded in quarters or thirds.

The Importance of Putting Yourself in the Picture

Way back at the beginning, I talked about how my mom died young and the many ways it devastated me. One of the lasting pains is that I have almost no photos of my mom. I have four, to be exact. She was never in the pictures! She always took pictures of my brother, me, my dad and my grandpa. She'd wave us away and say she didn't look her best or that she felt fat. How I have longed for more pictures, both of her and *with* her.

Do you find yourself behind the camera, capturing moments of your family, but never stepping in front of the lens? Yes, you're the one making the magic happen—wrapping the presents, organizing the vacations and making sure everyone's needs are met. But when it comes time to take a picture, you suddenly step back, unwilling to be included because you're worried about how you look or how tired you feel.

This is a metaphor for how many of us live our lives. We're always behind the scenes, ensuring everything runs smoothly, but rarely giving ourselves permission to be part of the moment. It's time to change that. Put yourself in the picture—not just literally, but figuratively as well. You deserve to be part of the memories, part of the experiences and part of the narrative.

Too often, we shy away from being seen. We don't want to capture our tired faces or puffy eyes. But guess what? Your kids don't notice those things. They won't look back on these photos and see a mom with eye bags or a muffin top; they'll see a mom who was present, who was there with them, loving them and creating memories. That's what matters.

Putting yourself in the picture is an act of self-care. It's a way of saying, "I matter, too." You don't need to be perfect. You just need to be there. So next time someone pulls out a camera, don't step aside. Smile, take a deep breath and know that you belong in the frame.

You deserve to be in the middle of the picture—not just in the literal sense, but in life. You deserve to prioritize yourself, to make choices that feel good for you and to live a satisfied life that aligns with your values.

Self-care isn't selfish; it's essential. It allows you to show up fully for the people you love, to thrive in your work and personal life and to find satisfaction on your own terms. Whether it's rejecting expectations, nurturing your most important relationships or putting yourself in the picture, remember that taking care of yourself is the first step toward satisfaction—and the first step toward enjoying everyone else.

You've got this.

Satisfaction Journal

What does self-care look like for you right now?

Practical Step: Reflect on the ways you currently practice self-care. Write down one small change you could make to align your self-care with what truly satisfies you—whether it's setting boundaries, prioritizing rest or creating more moments of joy.

How can you redefine self-care beyond indulgence?

Practical Step: List three non-indulgent ways to practice self-care, like saying "no," stepping outside for a quiet moment or delegating a task. Choose one to implement this week and reflect on its impact.

How can you be more present in your relationships?

Practical Step: Think of a recent moment when you felt disconnected from your partner, kids or loved ones. Write down one way to pause, reset and connect more meaningfully—whether it's putting down your phone, asking a thoughtful question or simply listening.

What does your inner voice say to you, and how can it be kinder?

Practical Step: Write down three critical thoughts you often tell yourself. Next to each, replace it with a compassionate statement that acknowledges your effort and worth.

What does it mean to put yourself in the picture—literally and figuratively?

Practical Step: Plan one moment this week where you intentionally "put yourself in the picture"—whether it's joining a family photo, taking time for a meaningful activity or stepping into the spotlight at work or home.

How can you model self-care for those around you?

Practical Step: Identify one way your self-care practices could inspire or encourage others, like teaching your kids to value rest or showing your team the importance of boundaries. Write down one action you can take to lead by example.

As you close this book and step into the rhythm of your own life, remember this: Satisfaction is not a destination, it's a daily choice. It's found in the small moments where you prioritize what truly matters, courageously let go of expectations and offer yourself grace along the way.

May you find the strength to stand firm in your values, the wisdom to embrace joy in the journey and the boldness to claim the life that satisfies your soul. You have all you need within you to create a life that feels authentic, fulfilling and deeply connected to who you are.

So, here's to you—to your imperfect, beautiful and entirely unique path forward. May you live life fully, love deeply and find the kind of satisfaction that lingers long after the last page is turned.

With my best wishes and unwavering belief in your journey,

Denise Brown

ACKNOWLEDGMENTS

T his book has been a journey shaped by the many people who have touched my life.

I've been blessed with the support of my soul sisters—Marianne, who walked alongside me since we met in prenatal yoga 21 years ago, daring to be different together, and Jessica, whose European sensibility and wisdom have shown me how to raise confident, competent teenagers as the older sister I always needed.

The Cedar Street Crowd—Steph and Jenny, my extended family. Through shared dinners and endless support, you taught me that community is family. My boys had three dads instead of one, and Halloween has never been the same.

I've also been shaped by the incredible women of influence in my life. Mrs. Fernelius, my high school English teacher, was a stand-in mom when I needed one and taught me the power and specificity of words. Ruthie Kurpinski, the fairy grandma to my boys, became a dear friend and enriched our lives with her nurturing spirit. Jean Oxton, my kids' preschool teacher, showed me that independence and play are vital, a lesson that became a cornerstone of my leadership style.

To my dad, who made me breakfast in the '70s when that wasn't a "dad" thing to do, showing me what real partnership looks like. Your love and support have shaped who I am today.

I can't forget my Sequoia Hospital family—Cathy, John, George and Kristin. You helped me become the best doctor I could be while allowing me the time I needed with my family. Your guidance and friendship have been invaluable.

Saving the best for last: Alex, Will and Hank—you are the reason for this book. Alex, you've been both the eye of the storm and the wind beneath my wings. Your confidence in me has been utterly steadfast, unwavering and inherently supportive. I couldn't have done this without you.

About the Author

Denise S. Brown, MD, is a transformative leader with over three decades of experience in the healthcare industry. As a former CEO and Chief Strategy Officer, she has consistently driven organizational growth and led strategic initiatives in clinical settings. With 25 years as a practicing physician, Denise's clinical insights uniquely inform her strategic approaches to leadership and innovation. A respected author and mentor, Denise's work focuses on empowering women leaders in healthcare and beyond. Her book offers practical guidance for women navigating the intersection of personal decisions and professional achievements. Drawing from her own career journey, she inspires others to redefine success on their own terms.

Denise holds an MD from The University of Chicago's Pritzker School of Medicine, with residency training at Stanford and Vanderbilt. She balances her demanding career with a rich family life. Married to Alex, her childhood sweetheart, for 28 years, Denise is a mother to Will and Hank, who both still enjoy hanging out with her (sometimes!). Her strategic expertise continues to shape the future of women in leadership through her work as a speaker, advisor and board member.

ABOUT THE PUBLISHER

Legacy Launch Pad is a boutique publishing company that works with entrepreneurs from all over the world.

For more information about Legacy Launch Pad Publishing, go to: www.legacylaunchpadpub.com.

Download the Fairy God Doctor's daily prescription for a good life by scanning the QR code below:

ENDNOTES

[1] Søren Kierkegaard, *Journals IV A 164* (1843).

[2] Daniel H. Pink, *Drive: The Surprising Truth About What Motivates Us* (New York: Riverhead Books, 2009).

[3] Christina Wallace, *The Portfolio Life: How to Future-Proof Your Career, Avoid Burnout, and Build a Life Bigger than Your Business Card* (New York: Hachette Go, 2023).

[4] Duckworth, Angela. *Grit: The Power of Passion and Perseverance* (Scribner, 2016).

[5] Brown, B. *Rising Strong* (New York: Spiegel & Grau, 2015).

[6] Taleb, N. N. *Antifragile: Things That Gain from Disorder* (New York: Random House, 2012).

[7] Frizzell, N. *The Panic Years* (London: Bantam Press, 2021).

[8] Frizzell, N. *The Panic Years* (London: Bantam Press, 2021).

[9] https://www.ericaberman.ca/

[10] Eyal, Nir. *Indistractable: How to Control Your Attention and Choose Your Life* (BenBella Books, 2019).

[11] https://www.merriam-webster.com/dictionary/dictionary

[12] Loomans, D. (1994). *Full Esteem Ahead: 100 Ways to Build Self-Esteem in Children and Adults*. H J Kramer.

[13] Paychex. (n.d.). *What is a sabbatical leave policy?* Paychex. Retrieved January 14, 2025, from https://www.paychex.com/articles/human-resources/what-is-sabbatical-policy.